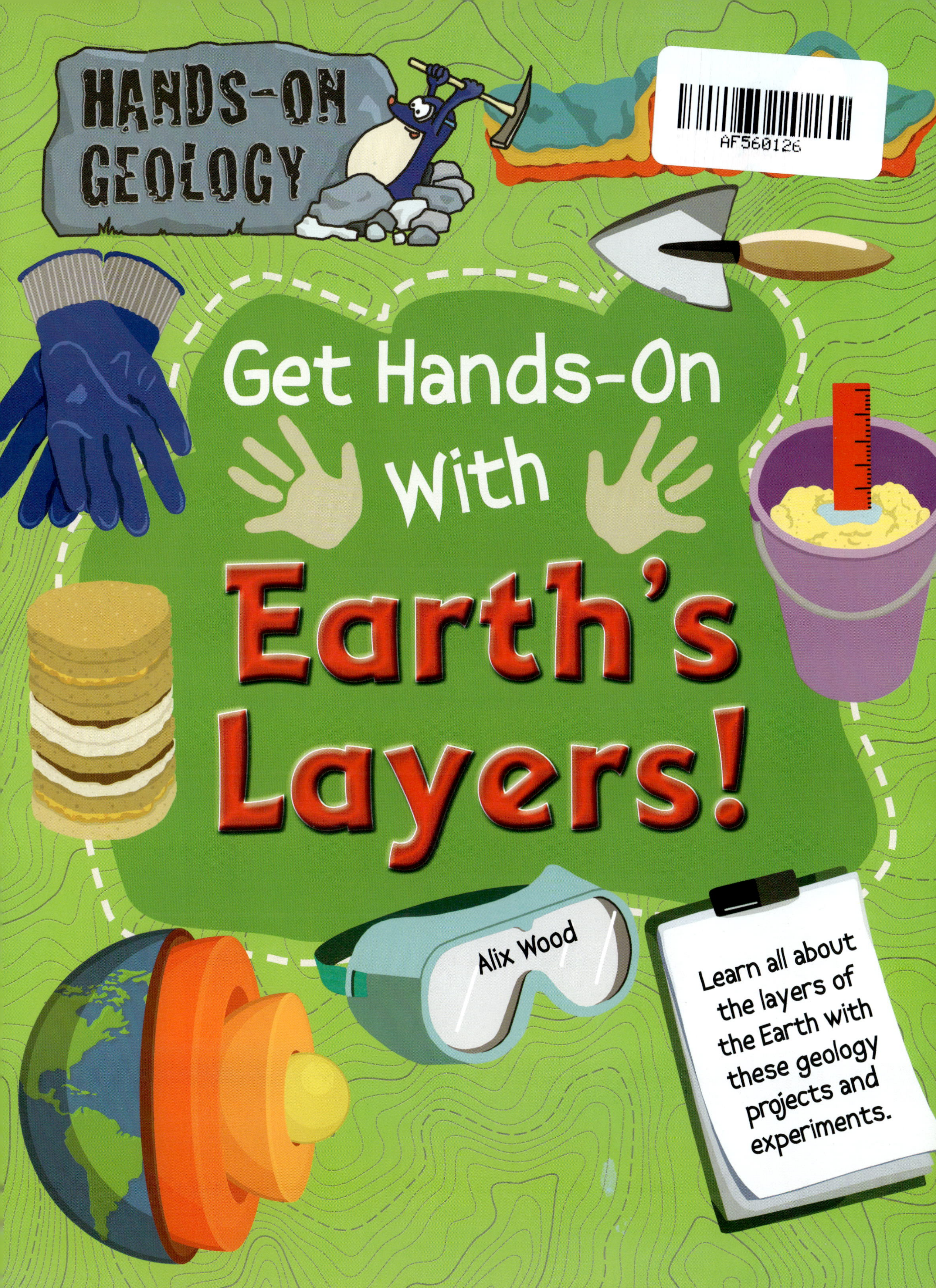

HANDS-ON GEOLOGY
Get Hands-On With
Earth's Layers!
Alix Wood
Learn all about the layers of the Earth with these geology projects and experiments.

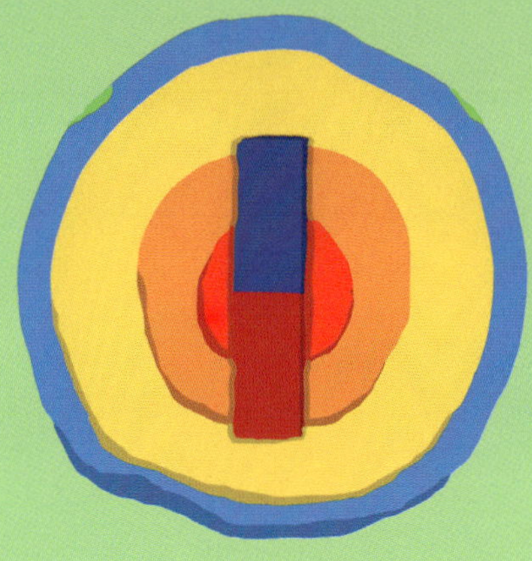

Published and Distributed in India by Scholastic India Pvt. Ltd.

Produced by Alix Wood Books
Designed by Alix Wood
Editor: Eloise Macgregor

Consultant: Kate Spencer, Professor of Environmental Geochemistry

Photo credits:
Cover bottom centre, 1 bottom left and right, 4 bottom, 7, 11, 14 top three, 15 top right, 16 top, 18 top and middle, 19 top, 20 top and middle, 21 top four, 22, 23 top, 26, 28 top © AdobeStock Images; 4 top © Hendric Stattmann/ public domain; 12 top public domain; 27 © USAF Sr. Airman Joshua Strag/ public domain; all other illustrations © Alix Wood

36 top, 38, 40, 41, 42 top, 43 top, 44, 46 top, 47 top, 50 bottom, 51 top, 52 bottom, 54 top, 56 top and bottom, 60 top, 61 top © AdobeStock Images; all other illustrations @ Alix Wood

Printed in India by Saurabh Printers Pvt. Ltd.
First edition: 2021
This Reprint Edition: May 2024

ISBN 978-93-5954-309-3

Contents

Living On An Onion 4

How Thick Is Each Layer? 6

Explore Earth's Layers 8

The Earth's Crust 10

Oceanic Crust 12

Continental Crust 14

Finding Treasure Underground 16

The Mantle 18

Moving Layers 20

The Lower Mantle 22

The Outer Core 24

How the Outer Core Affects Life on Earth's Crust 26

The Inner Core 28

Glossary 30

Further Information 31

Index 32

Living On An Onion

Our planet, Earth, is made up of layers, a little like an onion. We live on the thin outer layer, known as the crust. Underneath the crust the layers are very different. The temperature gets hotter and the pressure gets higher as you get closer to the centre of the Earth.

The deepest canyons barely make a dent in the Earth's crust. The Grand Canyon is just one mile (1.6 km) deep.

Beneath the rocky crust, the extreme temperatures in the other layers are hot enough to melt rock!

Think About This...

The deepest man-made hole, the Kola Superdeep Borehole, is 7.45 miles (12 km) deep. Why do you think people have not drilled any deeper?

How Did Earth's Layers Form?

The Earth formed around 4.6 billion years ago. Clouds of gas and dust in the **galaxy** began forming a ball. The larger the ball got, the more the force of **gravity** pulled objects towards it. Earth became a giant, hot ball of melted rock.

Slowly, Earth started to cool down. As the spinning Earth cooled, the denser materials, such as the metals nickel and iron, sank to the centre and formed the core. The lighter materials, like silica and aluminium rose to the top and formed the crust. The crust cooled and hardened. Deep underground, the Earth is still full of melted hot rock.

HANDS-ON Make A Model Earth

You will need:

- some red, orange, yellow, blue and green plasticine (you can use coloured marzipan if you like)
- a board to roll your shapes on
- a plastic knife

Keep your model Earth. You will use it later in the book.

For your core, take a small lump of red plasticine. Roll it into a ball.

To make the outer core, press a larger lump of orange plasticine into a rough circle. Wrap it around the core and mould it until it covers the core entirely. Repeat the same process, using a circle of yellow plasticine, for your mantle.

Now create the Earth's crust. Make an even larger thin circle of blue plasticine to wrap around your model. Then take some little bits of green plasticine and create some areas of land. You could look at a globe if you want to make it really accurate.

Using the plastic knife, cut your Earth model in half to reveal the layers. You can push the halves together and separate them when you like.

How Thick Is Each Layer?

Compared to the total size of our planet, the tallest mountains and deepest canyons on Earth's crust are just tiny bumps and scratches! The average distance from the centre of Earth's core to the surface is around 3,967 miles (6385 km). Although the core and mantle are almost the same thickness as each other, the core makes up only 15 per cent of Earth's volume. The mantle makes up 84 per cent, and the crust makes up 1 per cent.

Think About This...

If they are around the same thickness, why do you think the core makes up much less volume of the Earth than the mantle?

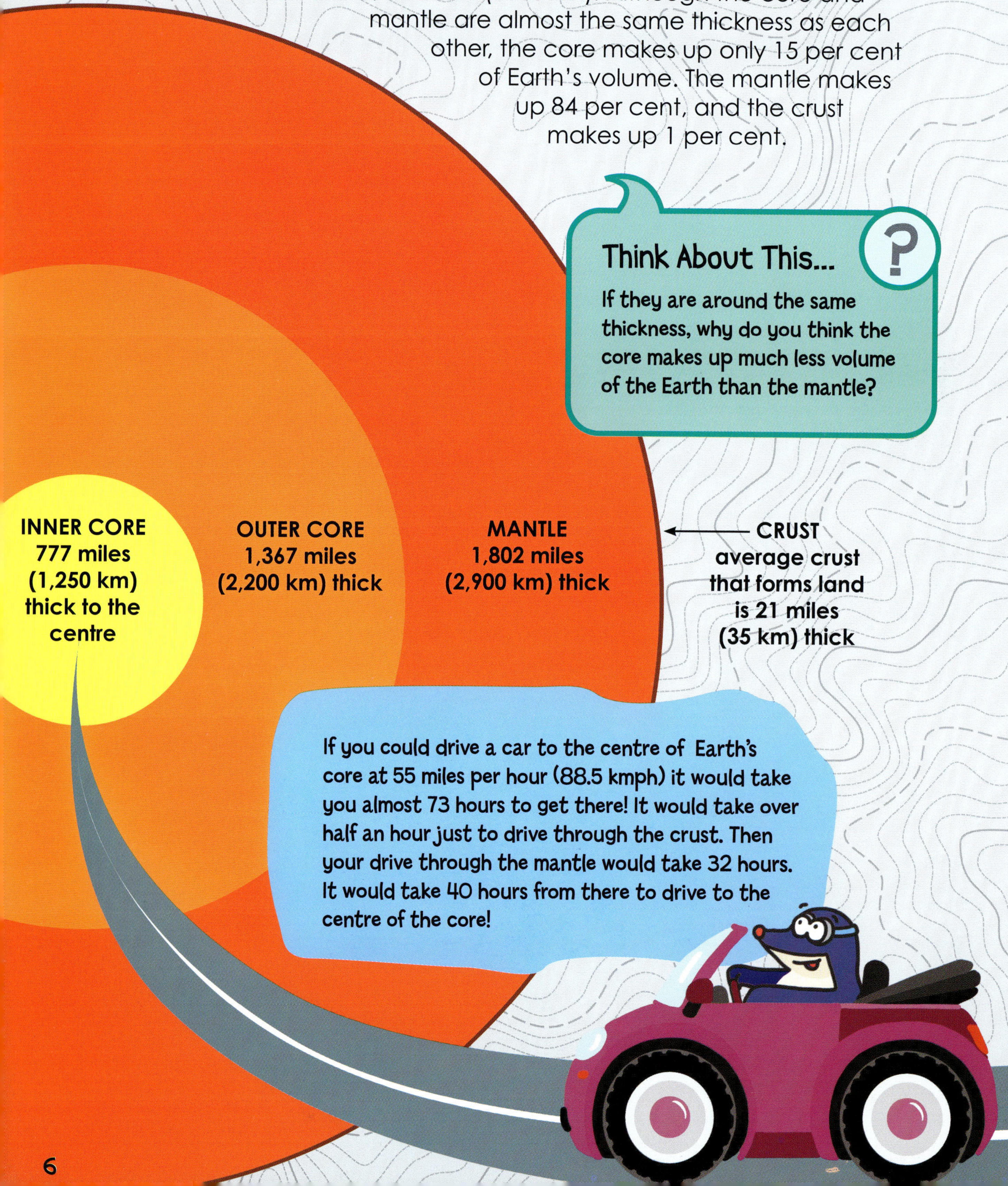

INNER CORE
777 miles (1,250 km) thick to the centre

OUTER CORE
1,367 miles (2,200 km) thick

MANTLE
1,802 miles (2,900 km) thick

CRUST
average crust that forms land is 21 miles (35 km) thick

If you could drive a car to the centre of Earth's core at 55 miles per hour (88.5 kmph) it would take you almost 73 hours to get there! It would take over half an hour just to drive through the crust. Then your drive through the mantle would take 32 hours. It would take 40 hours from there to drive to the centre of the core!

BE A GEOLOGIST
Make a Scale Model Of Earth's Layers

You Will Need:

- a pair of compasses
- a pencil
- a centimetre ruler
- some coloured card
- scissors
- a pin
- a paper fastener

How To Make the Model:

If you have never used compasses. ask an adult to help you. For the inner core, adjust your compass opening to measure 1.25 cm, using the ruler. Poke the point of the compass into the middle of some yellow card. Holding the pointed end still, carefully rotate the pencil to draw your circle. Then cut it out. Do this with a different colour for each layer.

The compass measurements you need are:

Outer core 3.45 cm
Mantle 6.35 cm
Crust and Earth 6.38 cm

To cut the pizza slice from the Earth layer, draw a small circle around the compass hole. Draw two straight lines at right angles from that circle to the edge. Cut away the slice, carefully cutting around the little circle.

Poke a paper fastener through the compass holes in this order: Earth, inner core, outer core, mantle, crust. Decorate your Earth and label the layers. Write things you know about each layer on the hidden areas. Then you can turn your layers and reveal your facts!

HANDS-ON Chalk a Massive Earth!

You will need:

- a large area of pavement
- some pavement chalk
- a long piece of string
- a friend
- a centimetre tape measure

Use the same numbers as above to make a giant chalk Earth on your pavement. Just move the **decimal points** one place. Tie some chalk to one end of the string. For the inner core, measure out 12.5 cm of string and tie a knot. Ask a friend to stand on the knot. Pull the string taut and draw around with the chalk. Repeat with these measurements: Outer core 34.5 cm, Mantle 63.5 cm, Crust 63.8 cm.

Explore Earth's Layers

It's a strange fact that astronauts can travel to the Moon, but we cannot explore deep inside our own planet. Why? If we travelled toward the centre of Earth we would quickly die of the extreme heat. The temperature at Earth's centre is as hot as the surface of the Sun.

The pressure also increases because of the force of gravity. At Earth's core, the pressure is three and a half million times greater than at Earth's surface! Any vehicle we made would not survive those extreme conditions.

How Do We Know What It Is Like?

Even though we have never explored deep inside Earth, we do know quite a bit about it. How? Geologists record and study **seismic waves**. Seismic waves are caused by things like **earthquakes**, explosions, and the movement of the oceans.

There are two types of seismic wave. Shear waves (**S-waves**) can travel through solids but not liquids. Pressure waves (**P-waves**) can move through both liquids and solids. Geologists use an instrument known as a seismograph to record how waves move through the Earth. The results prove there must be different layers, containing different material.

Think About This...

If an S-wave is recorded on the opposite side of Earth from an earthquake, what does that tell you about the layers it has travelled through?

BE A GEOLOGIST
Exploring Earth's Seismic Waves

You Will Need:

- three or four friends
- an open space

The Geology:

Seismic waves carry energy away from the center of an earthquake to the surface. The speed of the waves depends on the type of wave and the type of materials they meet. Geologists can work out if the layers the waves travel through are solid or liquid.

How To Do The Experiment:

You and your friends stand in a line, one behind the other. Each of you represents an **atom**. With your hands out in front of you, and your arms straight, grip the shoulders of the person in front. Your grip represents the **bonds** that hold atoms together in a solid.

To mimic a pressure wave through a solid, ask the person at the back to firmly push the shoulders of the person in front. Everyone in the line should move forwards, as energy is transferred from atom to atom through the bonds.

To mimic a pressure wave through a liquid, ungrip each other. Keep your arms raised, just behind the shoulders. When the person at the back pushes, the wave should still be transferred down the line.

To mimic a shear wave through a solid, face forwards and interlock arms. Ask a person at one end to step quickly forward and then back. This should produce a wobble that goes all the way down the line.

To mimic a shear wave through liquid, unlink your arms. Now, when the end person moves back and forth it does not affect the others. Having no bonds means the energy can't travel through a shear wave.

The Earth's Crust

The crust is the outer later of the Earth. As Earth was forming, and starting to cool, **vapour** rose from the surface. The vapour fell back down to Earth as rain. Eventually that rain formed oceans. Some of the Earth's crust became land, and some was covered by sea.

Geologists think one large mass of land, known as Pangaea, split into the **continents** that we know today. We know Earth's continents changed because fossils of sea creatures have been found in places surrounded by land. Fossils of the same animals have also been found in separate continents, hinting that they were once joined.

Think About This...

Look at the map of present day continents. Can you see how some of them might fit together like a jigsaw?

Pangaea

Present day

Two types of crust

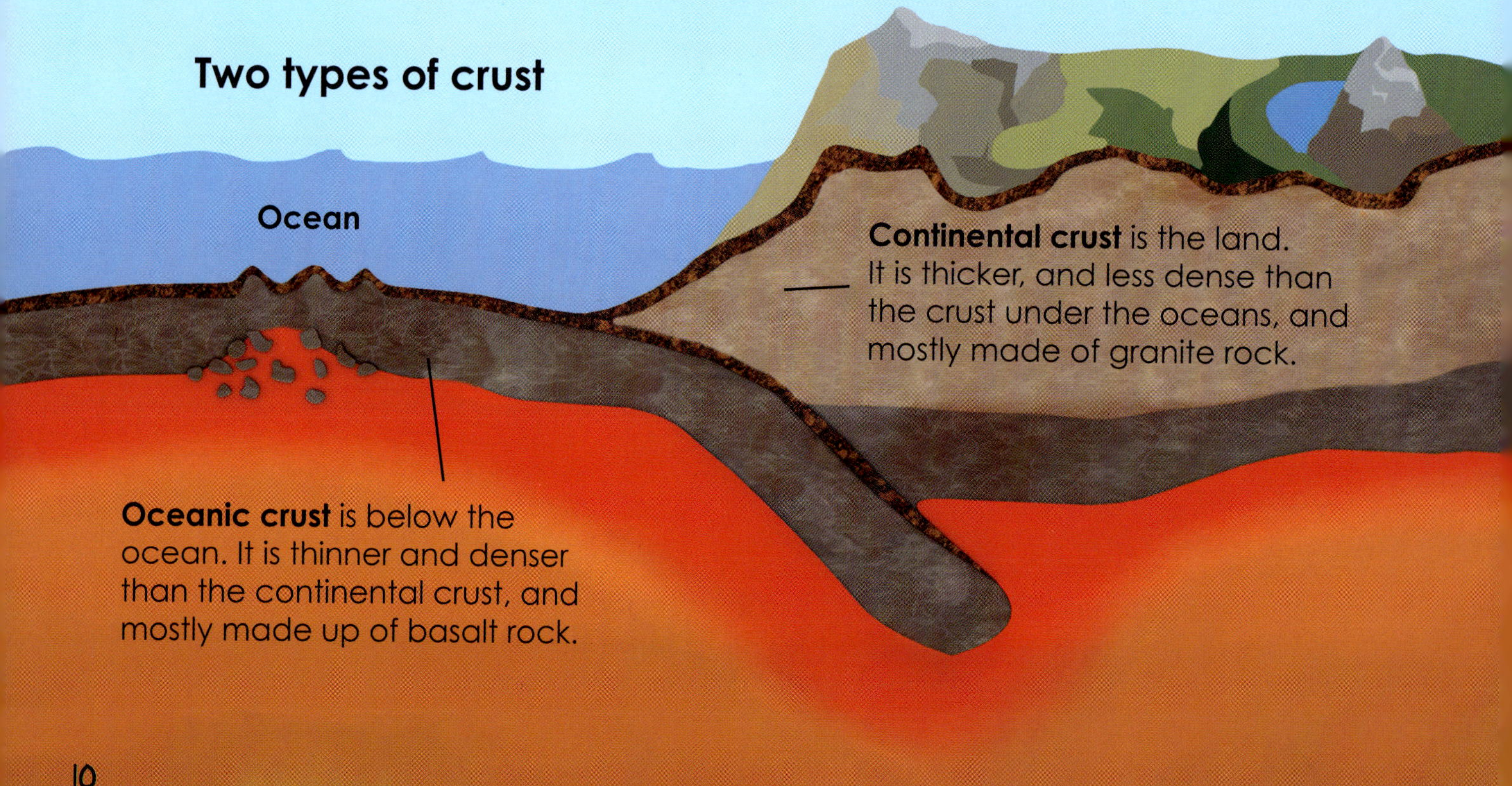

Ocean

Continental crust is the land. It is thicker, and less dense than the crust under the oceans, and mostly made of granite rock.

Oceanic crust is below the ocean. It is thinner and denser than the continental crust, and mostly made up of basalt rock.

HANDS-ON How The Oceans Formed

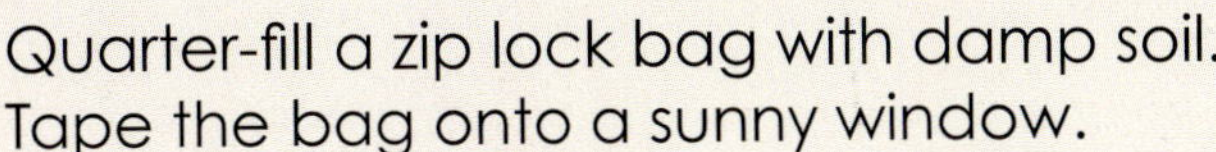

You will need:
- a small zip lock bag
- masking tape
- some damp soil

Quarter-fill a zip lock bag with damp soil. Tape the bag onto a sunny window.

Observe what happens over a few days. As the Sun heats the soil, the water will **evaporate** into a vapour. As the vapour cools, it forms clouds. When the clouds are full, the water falls as rain. This same process happened as Earth formed. Steam rose from the hot Earth, cooled, and fell as rain, forming the oceans.

BE A GEOLOGIST
Explore How Continents Move

You Will Need:
- a chocolate bar with chewy layers
- a plastic knife
- a pencil and notepad
- a camera, if you have one

The Geology:
The layers of your candy bar represent the layers of the Earth. The cracks you made represent fault lines in the Earth's crust. A fault line is a long crack in the surface of Earth. Earthquakes usually occur along fault lines.

How To Do The Experiment
Using a plastic knife, make small cracks in the chocolate bar's outer layer. Draw or photograph each stage of this experiment.

Pull the ends of the bar apart. Gaps should open up at the cracks.

Push the ends of the bar together. This represents what a pressure wave might do to cracks in Earth's crust.

Now twist the ends in opposite directions. This represents what a shear wave would do.

When events such as earthquakes occur, the shifts in the Earth's core affect the Earth's crust.

Oceanic Crust

The oceanic crust is thinner, younger and denser than crust under land. It is similar, though. It is made up of layers, and has mountains, valleys, plains and volcanoes. Geologists study oceanic crust by examining rock samples, drilling into the ocean floor and exploring the ocean bed in underwater vehicles. They also study **ophiolite**. Ophiolite is oceanic crust that has been forced up above sea level. It is easier to study than crust at the bottom of the ocean!

Ophiolite found in the Himalayas and the Alps (above) show rock from these mountain ranges were once part of an ocean floor.

Earth's crust is divided into plates. When two plates of oceanic crust move apart, molten **lava** flows up through the gap, creating new crust. Older oceanic crust is pushed outward and sinks down trenches into the mantle, This is known as **subduction**. The sunken rock is then recycled into lava. Most oceanic lava creates basalt rock. Basalt is made from tiny grains, which makes it very dense.

HANDS-ON Understanding Plates

You will need:

- peanut butter
- a wooden spoon
- two rectangular crackers
- a plate

Mimic when two plates under the ocean move away from each other. Spoon a thick layer of peanut butter onto the plate. Rest two crackers on the surface. The crackers are the plates of your oceanic crust. The peanut butter is the mantle. Press down a little on each cracker and gently pull them apart. Observe what happens. You should see some of the mantle ooze up through the gap, creating new crust or maybe even a peanut butter island! Slide one cracker under the other. This mimics the older crust being forced down into a trench.

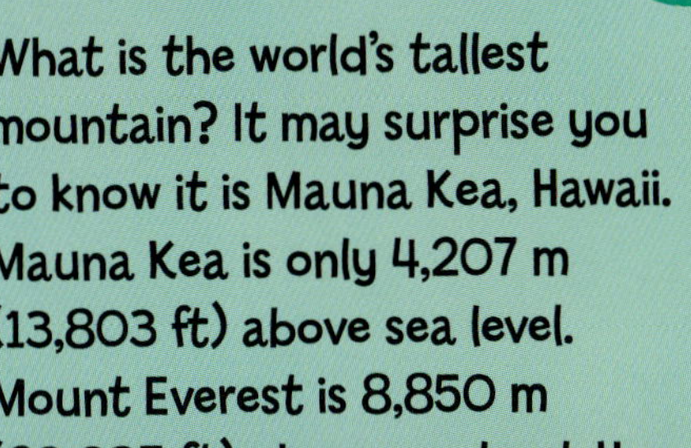

Think About This...

What is the world's tallest mountain? It may surprise you to know it is Mauna Kea, Hawaii. Mauna Kea is only 4,207 m (13,803 ft) above sea level. Mount Everest is 8,850 m (29,035 ft) above sea level. How do you think Mauna Kea can be taller than Mount Everest?

The Atlantic Ocean is actually getting bigger. The crust beneath the Atlantic is creating new rock faster than it is losing older rock. It is growing about 2.5 cm (one inch) per year. The Pacific Ocean is getting smaller. The older crust is sinking into a very deep trench, the Mariana Trench, faster than lava can create new rock.

The Moho

The boundary between the mantle and crust is known as the **Moho** after Andrija Mohorovicic, a Croatian scientist who discovered it. He realized the speed of seismic waves changed with the density of the material they moved through. This knowledge led scientists to be able to measure the depth of the crust, the point where less dense rock met the more dense mantle.

Continental Crust

About 40 per cent of Earth's surface is continental crust. Continental crust is older than oceanic crust. It is lighter, so it doesn't sink into the mantle and renew itself like oceanic crust does. Some crust has been on the surface for almost as long as our planet has existed. Even rock on the continental crust renews itself, though, through the rock cycle.

Three types of rock make up Earth's crust:

Igneous rock forms when hot molten rock called **magma** cools. Granite and basalt are igneous rock.

Metamorphic rock forms from rock changed by heat and pressure deep under the surface of Earth. Slate and marble are metamorphic rock.

Sedimentary rock forms as mountains **erode** and pieces of worn rock get carried into rivers and oceans. The pieces get compressed and form rock. Sandstone and shale are sedimentary rocks.

The Rock Cycle

Forces inside Earth slowly move underground igneous and metamorphic rock to the surface, where it **weathers** and erodes. Rock fragments sink down, and get heated and pressed into sedimentary rock, or melted to form magma which is forced to the surface —to start the cycle over again!

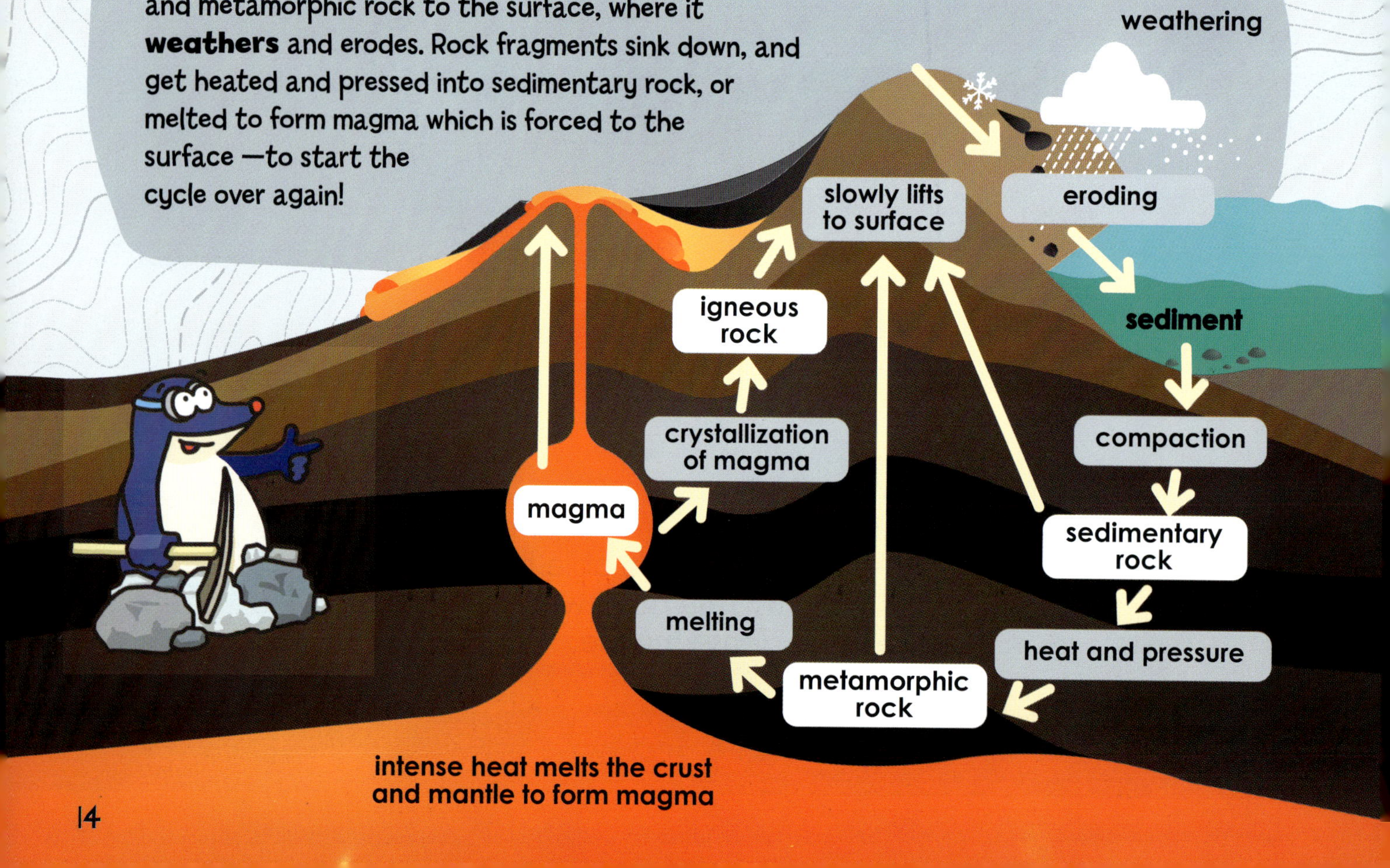

weathering

slowly lifts to surface

eroding

igneous rock

sediment

crystallization of magma

compaction

magma

sedimentary rock

melting

heat and pressure

metamorphic rock

intense heat melts the crust and mantle to form magma

Layers Upon Layers

Geologists have a law that says any rock layer underneath another layer must be older than the one above it.

Geologists sometimes draw a diagram of an area's rock layers. This helps them remember where each rock type was in relation to other layers, and helps age each layer of rock.

Think About This...

Why do you think the layers at the top are the youngest?

BE A GEOLOGIST
Make and Take a Rock Sample

You Will Need:

- several different types of bread
- some sandwich spreads
- a plastic beaker
- a spoon
- a notepad and pencil
- a camera if you have one

The Geology:

A **core sample** is taken using a drill-like tool. The tool removes a circular sample of a rock **formation** for geologists to study. A formation is a group of rock layers.

How To Make It

Recreate a rock formation using layers of bread. You could recreate the photograph above. Perhaps use white bread for sandstone, and brown bread for basalt? For thin layers, use some sandwich spread. Try to get the thickness, texture and colour as accurate as you can in your model.

To take a core sample, place an upturned beaker on your model. Press down hard. Lift the beaker. If your core sample gets stuck in the beaker, gently prise it out using a spoon. Draw or photograph your core sample. Make a key showing what each layer represents.

Key
brown bread = basalt
white bread = sandstone
peanut butter = sediment
meat paste = granite

Finding Treasure Underground

Treasure comes in many forms. Geologists help find rock containing precious gems or metals such as diamonds, or gold. They also help find precious **resources** such as water for us to drink; or coal, oil or gas to power things. All of these resources can be found underground in Earth's crust.

Water seeps through surface rock and is stored between layers of rock in areas known as **aquifers**. Fossil fuels, such as coal, form when **microorganisms** die, fall to the ocean floor and become buried. Over millions of years gas, oil or coal forms, depending on the temperature and pressure. How do geologists know where to find these hidden underground resources? They drill holes and study core samples. If the resource is found in a core sample, then it may be worth digging a mine or well there.

HANDS-ON

The Water Table

You will need:

- a bucket and spade
- sand and water
- a ruler, notepad and pencil

Quarter-fill a bucket with water. Gradually add sand until a layer covers the water. To find your water table, dig a hole until you reach a puddle. Record the height of the water level. Fill your hole back in and leave the bucket in a sunny, dry spot. Record the level again after a couple of days. Has it changed?

Think About This...

Aquifers trap water between two layers of impermeable rock. What do you think "impermeable" means?

The water table is the level below which the soil is completely full of water. It can rise and fall, depending on rainfall and evaporation by the Sun.

BE A GEOLOGIST
The Geological Survey Game

You Will Need:

- a friend
- different coloured modelling clay
- a straw or dried pasta tube
- a notepad and coloured pencils
- some toothpicks
- masking tape

The Geology:

Rock core samples tell us a lot about what rock layers are made from, and what we may find in them. Geologists will usually take samples from more than one spot.

How To Do The Experiment:

Create a model of Earth's crust, with hidden resources in the layers. Then challenge a friend to take core samples. Can they find the best place to drill for each resource?

Send your friend away while you set up the experiment. Take lumps of different colour modelling clay and create your Earth layers. Decide what colour each resource or rock layer will be. Draw a key in your notepad showing the colour and what it represents. To make the game work, you need each resource to only occur in certain areas, or be different thicknesses.

Make marker flags by wrapping masking tape around the top of some toothpicks. Number each flag.

Now, ask your friend to come in and do their survey. To take a sample, they should push the straw or dried pasta into the clay, and then lift it out. Gently squeeze or poke each core sample out of the tube and lay it on your notepad. Give each sample a number and write it next to it. Mark where each sample was taken using the correct numbered flag.

When they have completed their survey, ask if they can tell you the best spot to drill for each resource. Then gently lift up the clay layers to check if they were right!

The Mantle

As the Earth formed, the dense iron and nickel metals sank to the centre to form the core. Molten material surrounding the core formed the mantle. Over time, the mantle cooled and became more solid. The mantle makes up around 85 per cent of the Earth's weight. It has two main layers, the upper mantle and the lower mantle.

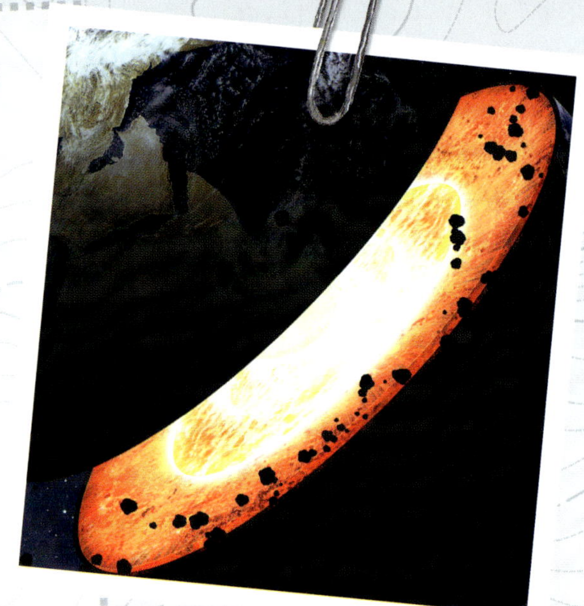

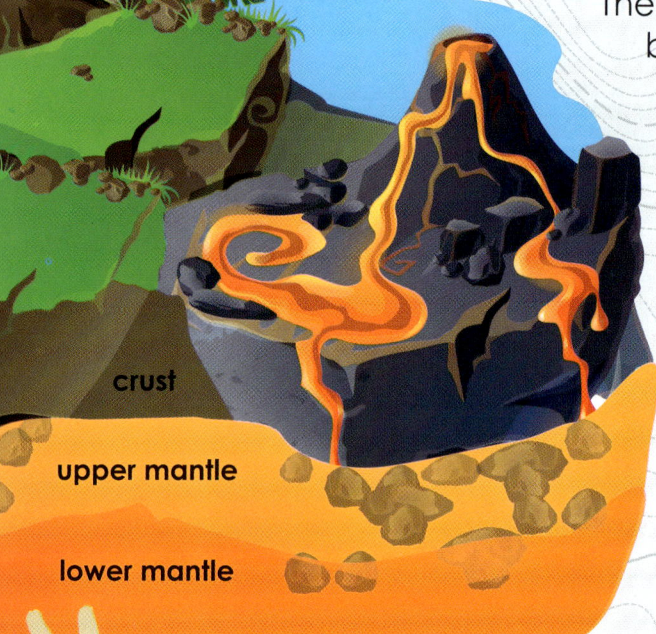

The Upper Mantle

The upper mantle is a thick layer of rock just beneath Earth's crust. Near the crust is cooler, so the rock there is firmer. The hotter, lower part has both solid and melted rock.

Movement in the mantle helps shape the landscape on Earth's crust. Large slabs of rock in the upper mantle, known as **tectonic plates**, float slightly on the partly liquid mantle. Tiny plate movements cause earthquakes, volcanic eruptions, form mountains, and cause the continents to slowly move.

HANDS-ON The Upper Mantle

You will need:

- a tray
- a heavy book
- five of six marbles
- a toy animal

Put some marbles on a tray. The marbles are your upper mantle. Place a book on the marbles. The book is your crust. Put a toy animal on the book and gently tap the tray to create an earthquake. Does the crust wobble a little? Did your animal fall over?

Think About This...

This map shows how Earth is divided into tectonic plates. Look at the shape of the plates and the shape of the areas of land. What do you notice?

BE A GEOLOGIST
Experiment With Tectonic Plates

You Will Need:

- a pie pan
- some water
- red or orange food colour
- a polystyrene cup
- cover the floor and wear old clothes

The Geology:

It may not seem like it, but the land beneath our feet is constantly moving. It only moves from between 2.5 to 15.2 cm (1 to 6 inches) a year, though! Even these tiny movements of the mantle can cause earthquakes and volcanoes, and form our mountains.

How To Make It

Fill the pie pan with 2.5 cm (1 inch) of water. Drop a little food colour into the water so it looks more like molten rock. Tear a polystyrene cup into several pieces. The pieces represent tectonic plates. Float them on the water.

Now experiment with the plates. Pull two pieces away from each other. Does molten rock fill the space between the plates? Gently bump two plates together. Could this push up the crust to form a mountain range? Or cause an earthquake?

Push one plate under another. Your coloured water may squirt upward. Did it behave a little like a volcano?

Moving Layers

Earth's moving tectonic plates are on the crust and the upper mantle, together known as the **lithosphere**. The plates move very slowly, but the tiny movements cause changes to life on the Earth's crust.

Earthquakes

Sometimes, the rough edges of two moving plates get stuck together. When the plates finally manage to slip apart, the sudden release of energy causes an earthquake. The surface where the plates slip is called a **fault**. The energy ripples outwards as seismic waves that shake the ground.

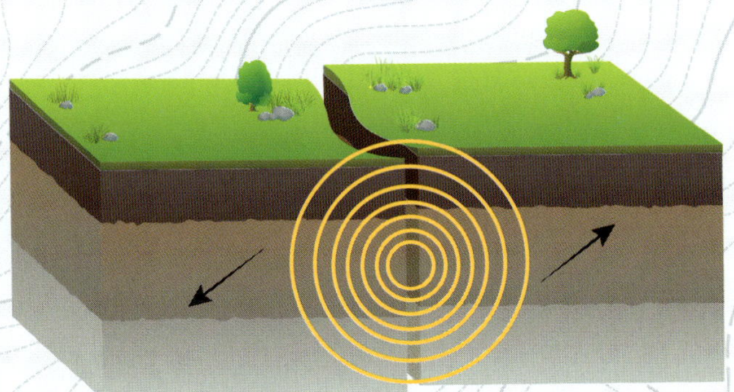

HANDS-ON Experiment With Faults

You will need:

- some cheese slices
- a few small coins

Layer four or five cheese slices on top of each other. Fold the stack in half until it splits. This split forms the edges of two tectonic plates. Place another whole cheese slice on top of the broken ones. This represents the plates sticking together.

Rest some coins on the top cheese slice. Holding a side of the stack in each hand, slowly slide your hands away from each other. Can you start to feel the tension on the top layer? That layer should suddenly give way and rip, causing your coins to wobble or fall, a little like buildings do in an earthquake.

Energy along a fault can build up and be stored for many years. Before and after a large earthquake there are often smaller earthquakes, known as foreshocks and aftershocks.

Making Mountains

Moving plates create mountains. If the plates push the crust slowly at an angle, it creates folds that form mountain ranges.

Plates can be forced up or down in blocks, forming fault-block mountains.

When magma is forced upward it creates volcanic mountains. If the magma doesn't break the surface, a dome mountain is formed.

folded mountain

fault block mountain

volcanic mountain

dome mountain

Think About This...

How do you think your region's mountains were formed?

BE A GEOLOGIST
Study Folded Mountain Ranges

You Will Need:

- several towels
- a friend to help you
- a camera if you have one
- a notebook and pencil

The Geology:

Your hands act like the force of moving tectonics plates. There are many different ways you can push the towels. Look at some mountain ranges. They all look slightly different for the same reason.

Make Your Mountain Range

Fold each towel in half. Lay them on top of each other to form layers. These layers represent layers of Earth's crust and upper mantle. Press a hand on each side of the towels and push them together so the towels form folds. You may want a friend to help you press one side while you press the other.

Photograph or draw your folded mountain formations. Experiment with different ways of pushing the towels together. Try only slightly pushing, or pushing at angles. Predict your result and then record what happens in your notebook.

The Lower Mantle

The lower mantle, like the upper mantle, is also made from magma. The lower mantle's magma is thicker and more solid, though. It is closer to the heat of Earth's core, so you would think its rock would be completely melted. Temperatures at the bottom of the lower mantle reach over 3,871 degrees Celsius (7,000 degrees Fahrenheit)! So why is its rock more solid?

The magma in the lower mantle is solid because of the huge pressure pushing down on it from above. Pressure in the lower mantle can reach 1.3 million times the pressure on the Earth's surface!

This pressure turns rock into minerals that could not be created on Earth's crust. How do we know what rock exists deep in the lower mantle? Geologists figure that out by looking at rock thrown out of erupting volcanoes. Volcanic rock comes from deep inside the mantle. Geologists know from this that the lower mantle is rich in iron, oxygen, silicon, aluminium and magnesium.

HANDS-ON

Volcanic Rock

See if you can find some volcanic rock at a local museum or rock shop. Or look at some pictures on geology websites. When magma cools and hardens on the surface it forms a type of rock that is almost glassy in texture. Obsidian is a type of rock formed in this way.

obsidian

When magma cools and hardens underground it forms grainy rocks such as granite and gabbro.

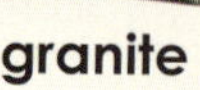

granite

BE A GEOLOGIST
How Pressure Affects the Mantle

You Will Need:

- a notepad and pencil
- measuring cup
- a plastic cup
- water
- corn flour
- a bowl
- a spoon

How To Do The Experiment:

Pour half a cup of water into the plastic cup. Gradually add corn flour, one tablespoon at a time. Stir the water after each spoonful. Keep adding corn flour until the mix becomes hard to stir.

Do you think you will be able to pour this mixture out of the cup? Try it. Tip the cup gently over the bowl and see if you can pour it. Make notes about how the mixture behaves when you pour it quickly, or slowly.

What happens to the mixture if you press it? Try to scrape the last bits out of the cup using the spoon. Does the mixture stay as a free-flowing liquid?

IMPORTANT–When you have finished your experiment, wrap the fluid in newspaper and put it in the trash. It will block your drains if you pour it down the sink.

The Geology:

In the lower mantle, the rock can be both liquid and solid. How can that be? A little like our corn flour experiment, the rock flows easily when it is not under pressure. When the rock is under pressure, it hardens.

The corn flour mixture is what is known as a **non-Newtonian fluid**. This fluid acts like a liquid when poured, but acts like a solid when a force is acting on it. Try grabbing some of the mixture. It will quickly harden under the pressure, and then slowly ooze out of your hands.

Think About This...

Quicksand is also a non-Newtonian fluid. It changes based on how much and at what speed a force is applied. What do you think the best way to escape quicksand would be? Try testing your theory using a plastic toy in your bowl.

The Outer Core

The outer core lies between the inner core and the mantle. It is made up of liquid iron and nickel. This layer of Earth plays an important part in protecting our planet from harmful **solar flares** and strong winds coming from the Sun. How can a layer deep under Earth's crust help protect us from the Sun?

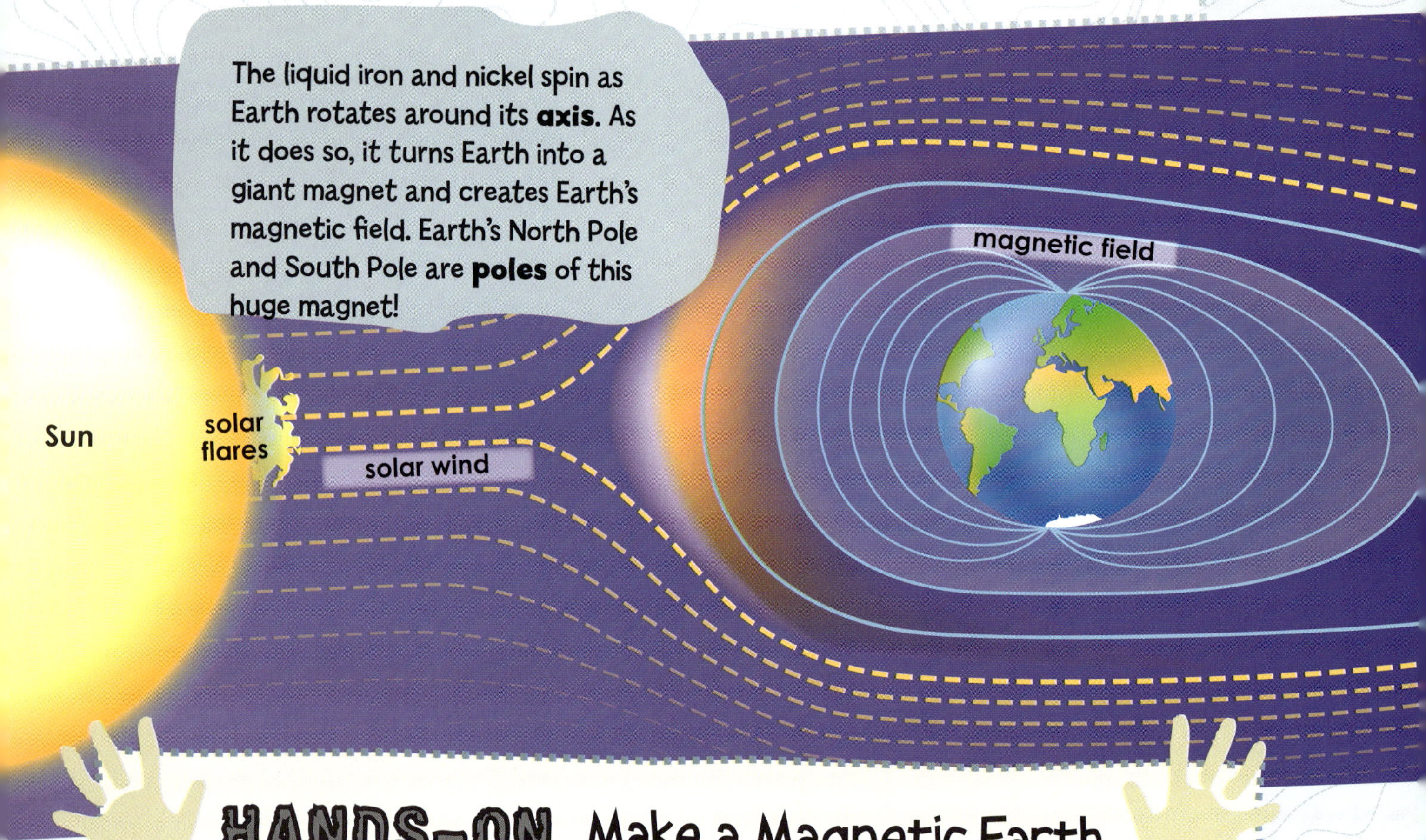

The liquid iron and nickel spin as Earth rotates around its **axis.** As it does so, it turns Earth into a giant magnet and creates Earth's magnetic field. Earth's North Pole and South Pole are **poles** of this huge magnet!

magnetic field

Sun

solar flares

solar wind

HANDS-ON Make a Magnetic Earth

You will need:

- a bar magnet
- a straw
- your model of Earth
- a small compass

Use the plasticine Earth you made on page 5 to make your magnetic Earth. Split your Earth in half. Press a bar magnet into one half from North to South. Press a straw in the other half. Mold your model closed again. Move your compass around the Earth and watch how the needle reacts. Did you put your bar magnet the right way round?

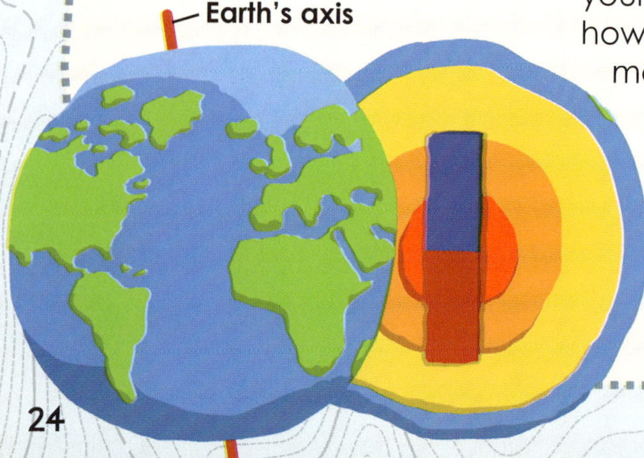

Earth's axis

Earth's magnetic field does not line up exactly with the axis. Magnetic poles move a little. The magnetic North Pole is close to Earth's axis now, but a hundred years ago, it was in Arctic Canada!

BE A GEOLOGIST
Looking At Magnetic Fields

You Will Need:

- a bar magnet
- iron filings (from hardware stores)
- a large piece of white paper
- pencil or pen
- a small compass

The Geology:

Even though magnetic fields are invisible, you can see them by seeing the effect they have on some objects. Field lines circle out from the North pole back to the South pole. Earth's magnetic field acts like a shield, protecting Earth from gases and particles that would harm our atmosphere.

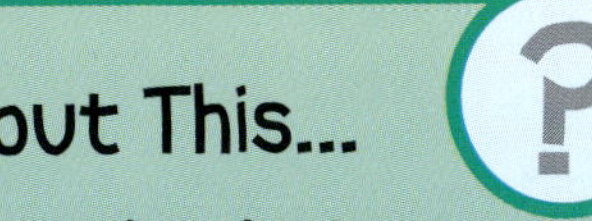

Think About This...

We believe migrating birds use magnetic fields to find their way!

How To Do The Experiment:

Place the bar magnet in the centre of a large piece of paper. Trace around the magnet and mark north and south.

Put the magnet back in position. Place the compass at the corner of one end. Mark a pencil line next to the compass arrow, in the direction it is pointing.

Move the compass so the base of its arrow points to the line you've just made. Mark a new line where the arrow is now pointing. Connect the lines to draw the magnetic field line. Repeat the process from different spots along the magnet to make more field lines.

Here's another cool way to see field lines. Place your magnet back in position, but under the paper. Sprinkle iron filings on the paper. Tap the paper gently. The filings will position themselves along the field lines you drew!

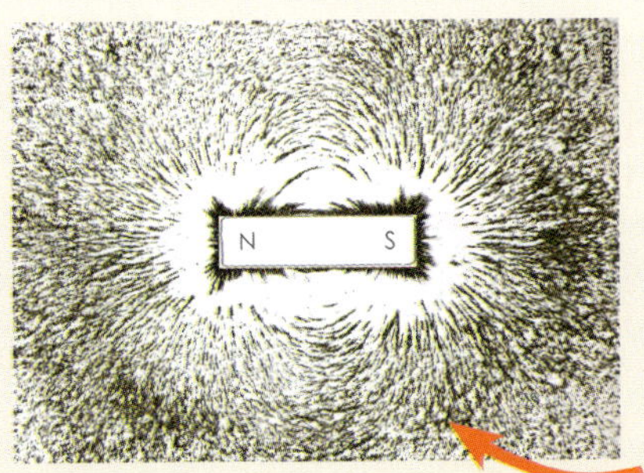

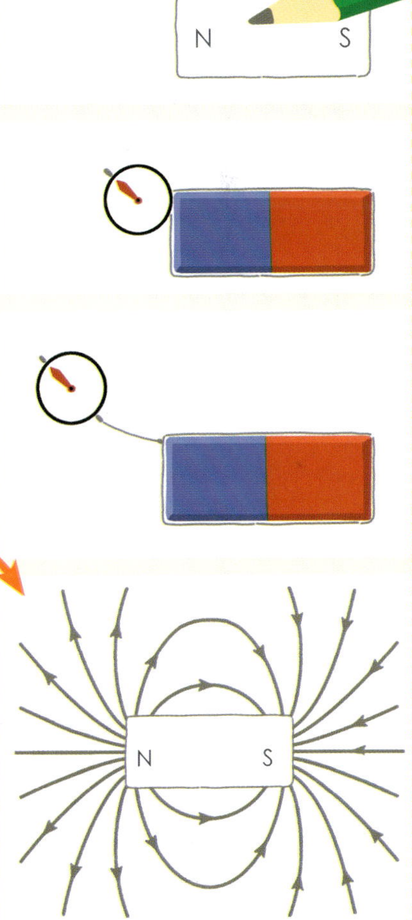

How The Outer Core Affects Life on Earth's Crust

Earth is gradually cooling and in billions of years time the outer core will become solid. Life on Earth would be impossible for many reasons, one of which is that a cold outer core would mean we would lose our important magnetic field.

The magnetic field helps protect Earth's atmosphere being blasted by solar wind.

The magnetic field helps birds and animals find their way around.

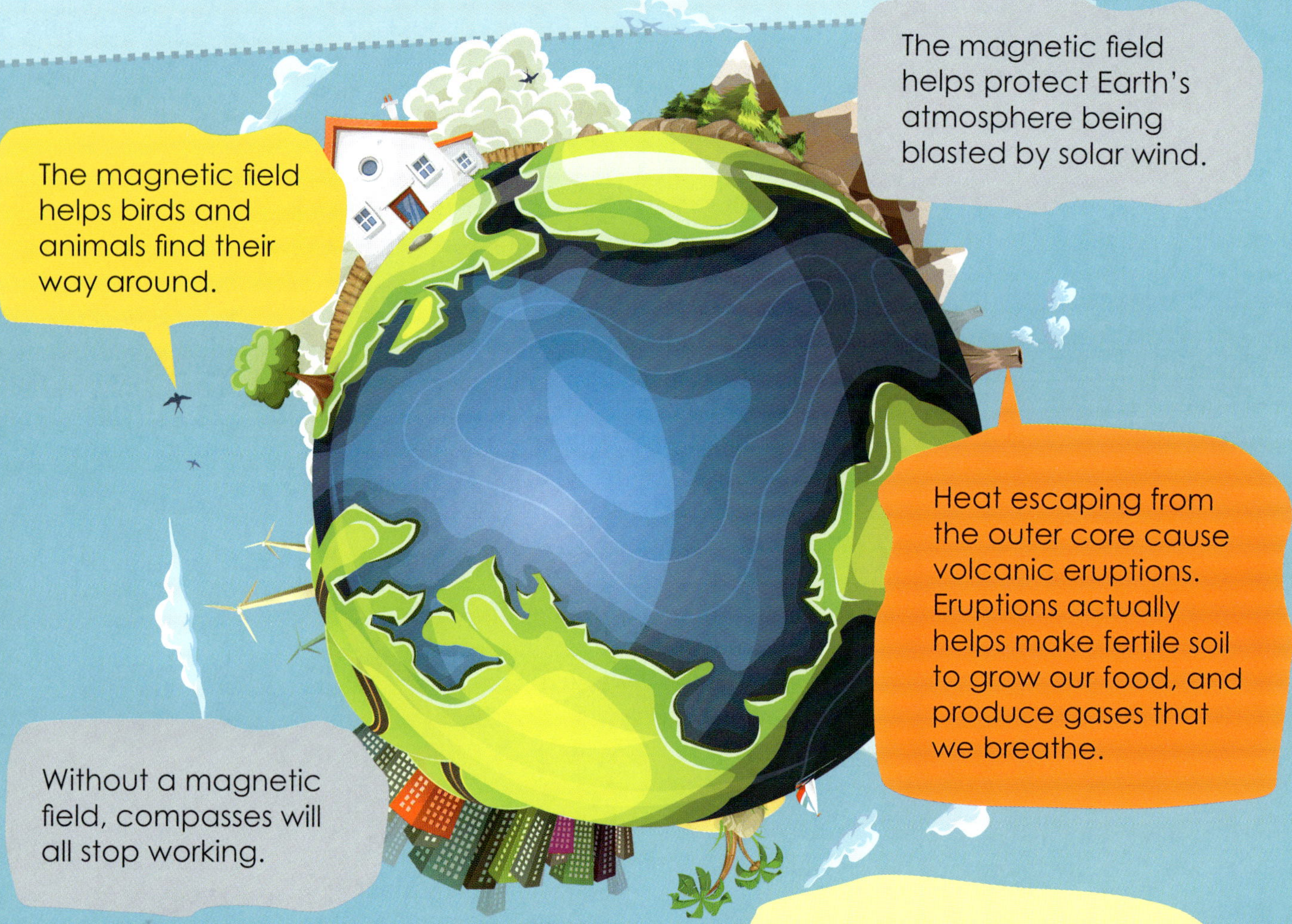

Heat escaping from the outer core cause volcanic eruptions. Eruptions actually helps make fertile soil to grow our food, and produce gases that we breathe.

Without a magnetic field, compasses will all stop working.

The magnetic field bounces dangerous radiation from the Sun back into space. Without it, our planet would overheat, and the oceans would disappear.

Think About This...

Saturn, Jupiter, Neptune and Uranus have magnetic fields even stronger than ours. What does that tell us about the inner layers of these planets?

When tiny particles from the Sun hit Earth's magnetic field the energy can cause amazing colours of light, called an **aurora**. Auroras occur most often around the North Pole (aurora borealis) and South Pole (aurora australis). Why? Earth's magnetic field guides the incoming particles toward the poles.

BE A GEOLOGIST
Make Your Own Compass

You Will Need:

- a magnet
- a needle
- piece of polystyrene
- large bowl of water
- a pencil and notebook

The Geology:

A compass needle will point North. Oddly, that has not always been true! Through time, the poles have reversed, so that North magnetic pole was South! These reversals are recorded in rocks with iron-bearing minerals. The minerals are like tiny magnets floating in the molten rock, and they align to the magnetic field. As the rock becomes solid, the minerals are still locked to that magnetic field.

How To Make a Compass:

Find a piece of polystyrene foam, perhaps a tray from some food packaging. Make sure it is clean. Cut a small piece of the foam and float it in a large bowl of water.

To magnetize your needle, rub the magnet along the needle around 50 times, in the same direction. Carefully place your needle on the foam in the bowl. Observe and record what happens.

Try moving the bowl around. Does your needle always point in the same direction? Do you know which direction it pointed?

The Inner Core

The inner core is the deepest layer on Earth. This metal ball made of iron and nickel is almost as hot as the surface of the Sun. Despite being so hot, the inner core is solid, because the pressure in the core is over a million times more than the pressure on Earth's surface.

The inner core spins faster than the rest of Earth. Scientists studying shock waves from nuclear explosions discovered the inner core moves a fraction faster than Earth's surface. Earth completes a turn on its axis about every 24 hours. As the inner core floats inside the molten outer core, it can turn at a different speed.

Earth's axis

If you stood on a spot along the Equator on the same day, two years running, the part of the inner core that was under you the first year would be 7.7 km (4.8 miles) away!

Think About This...

How long do you think it would take for the rotating inner core to overtake the crust?

HANDS-ON Model a Spinning Earth

You will need:

- a small lollipop
- a large marshmallow
- a teaspoon

The lollipop represents the solid inner core. The marshmallow represents the molten outer core.

Make a small slit in the top of the marshmallow using the end of a teaspoon. Carefully push the lollipop into the hole, so the lollipop is completely covered by the marshmallow.

Hold the stick between both palms. Slowly roll the lollipop stick between your hands. Observe what happens to the wobbly marshmallow. Do you think it spins at the same speed as the solid lollipop core?

Geologists know the inner core is solid from studying earthquakes' shear waves and seeing them travel from one side of Earth to the other. As we know shear waves cannot travel through a liquid, geologists are sure the inner core must be solid.

They also know the core is changing. The whole of Earth's core was molten when Earth first formed. As Earth cooled, a solid inner core was created. That solid area has been growing in size ever since, as the Earth continues to cool. The inner core grows about 1 mm (0.039 inches) a year.

BE A GEOLOGIST
Make an Edible Planet Earth!

You Will Need:

- a hard sweet
- a marshmallow
- chocolate chip ice cream
- chocolate shell sauce, chopped nuts or sprinkles
- a bowl
- a teaspoon
- a plastic knife

The Geology:

Each edible layer is quite a good representation of Earth's layers – and it tastes good!

How To Make The Layers:

To make your inner and outer core, push a hard sweet inside a marshmallow, just as you did for the spinning Earth.

For the mantle, make a large ball of ice cream. Cut it in half using the plastic knife. Scoop out enough space to fit your core inside. Then press the other half of the ice cream ball quickly back in place.

To make your Earth's crust, try using chocolate shell sauce. The sauce hardens when poured onto frozen ice cream. Put your Earth in the freezer for 15 minutes, then take it out again. Pour the sauce over the Earth and let it harden. Or, roll your ice cream ball in a bowl of sprinkles or chopped nuts.

Now you can eat your planet!

IMPORTANT–Be sure to warn people that there is a hard sweet hidden in the marshmallow. You can choke on sweets.

Glossary

aquifers an underground water-bearing layer of rock.

atom the smallest particle of an element, having all the characteristics of that element.

aurora broad bands of light that have a magnetic and electrical source and that appear in the sky at night.

axis a straight line about which a body or a geometric figure rotates.

bonds how atoms are held together.

continental crust the relatively thick part of the Earth's crust which forms the large land masses.

continents the great divisions of land.

core sample a cylindrical section of rocks, soils or sediments.

decimal points the dots in a decimal number.

earthquakes a shaking or trembling of a portion of the Earth's surface.

erode wear away by or as if by the action of water, wind or glacial ice.

evaporate to pass off or cause to pass off into vapour from a liquid state.

fault a break in the Earth's crust.

galaxy one of the very large groups of stars and other matter that are found throughout the universe.

gravity a force of attraction between particles or bodies that occurs because of their mass.

igneous rock rock formed by hardening of melted Earth.

lava molten rock coming from a volcano.

lithosphere the outer part of Earth made up of the crust and part of the mantle.

magma molten rock material inside Earth.

metamorphic rock a rock changed from its original form by temperature and pressure.

microorganisms extremely tiny organisms such as bacteria.

Moho the Mohorovicic discontinuity is the boundary layer between the Earth's crust and mantle whose depth varies.

non-Newtonian fluid a liquid that can change when under force to either more liquid or more solid.

oceanic crust the relatively thin part of the Earth's crust which underlies the ocean basins.

ophiolite a section of Earth's oceanic crust and the underlying upper mantle that has been uplifted and exposed above sea level.

poles one of two or more regions in a magnetized body at which the magnetism seems to be concentrated.

P-waves waves that shake the ground back and forth in the same direction and the opposite direction as the direction the wave is moving.

resources a usable stock or supply.

sediment material such as stones and sand deposited by water, wind or glaciers.

Sedimentary rock formed by or from sediment.

seismic waves elastic waves generated by an earthquake or an explosion.

solar flares a brief eruption of intense high-energy radiation from the Sun's surface.

subduction the sideways and downward movement of the edge of a plate of Earth's crust into the mantle beneath another plate.

S-waves waves that shake the ground back and forth perpendicular to the direction the wave is moving.

tectonic plates massive slabs of solid rock, generally made of both continental and oceanic lithosphere.

vapour a substance in the gaseous state.

weathers changes by the actions of the forces of nature.

Further Information

Museums and Places to Visit

Mining Museums. Your area may have a mining museum or visitor centre where you can find out about minerals that occur locally underground.

Science Museums will often have information about the geology of Earth, and may have exhibitions about earthquakes and volcanoes.

Useful Websites

This National Geographic Kids website has information about the features of each of Earth's layers.
https://www.natgeokids.com/uk/discover/geography/physical-geography/structure-of-the-earth/

The Science for Kids website is full of easy-to-understand facts and diagrams about Earth's layers.
https://www.scienceforkidsclub.com/earths-layers.html
This Science for Kids link has information about Earth's magnetism.
https://www.scienceforkidsclub.com/earths-magnetism.html/

Books to Read

Davis, Barbara, J. *Earth's Core and Crust*. New York, NY: Gareth Stevens Publishing, 2007.

Hutmacher, Kimberly. *Studying Our Earth, Inside and Out*. Vero Beach, FL: Rourke Educational Media, 2019.

Throp, Claire. *A Journey to the Center of the Earth*. Oxford, UK: Raintree, 2015.

Index

aftershocks 20
Alps, the 12
aluminium 5, 22
aquifers 16
Atlantic Ocean 13
atmosphere 25
atoms 9
aurora australis 27
aurora borealis 27
auroras 27
axis 24, 28

basalt 10, 12, 14, 15
bonds 9

canyons 4, 6
clouds 11
coal 16
compaction 14
compasses 25, 26, 27
continental crust 6, 10, 12, 14
continents 10, 18
core 4, 5, 6, 8, 18, 22, 28
core samples 15, 16, 17
crust 4, 5, 6, 7, 10, 11, 12, 13, 16, 17, 18, 20, 21, 24, 26, 28
crystallization 14

diamonds 16
dome mountains 21
drilling 12, 15, 16, 17

earthquakes 8, 9, 11, 18, 19, 20, 29
erosion 14
evaporation 16
Everest, Mount 13
Equator 28

fault block mountains 21
faults 20, 21
fault lines 11, 20
folded mountains 21
foreshocks 20
formations 15
fossils 10

gabbro 22
galaxy 5
gas 5, 16, 25, 26
gems 16
gold 16
Grand Canyon 4
grains 12, 22
granite 10, 14, 22
gravity 5

Himalayas, the 12

igneous rock 14
inner core 4, 5, 6, 7, 28, 29
iron 5, 18, 22, 24, 25, 27, 28

Jupiter 26

Kola Superdeep Borehole 4

lava 12, 13
liquids 8, 9, 18, 22, 23, 24, 29
lithosphere 20
lower mantle 18, 22, 23

magma 14, 21, 22
magnesium 22
magnetic fields 24, 25, 26, 27
magnetic poles 24, 25
mantle 4, 5, 6, 7, 12, 13, 14, 18, 22, 23, 24
marble 14
Mariana Trench 13
Maunu Kea 13
metals 16, 18
metamorphic rock 14
microorganisms 16
minerals 22, 27
mines 16
Moho, the 13
Mohorovicic, Andrija 13
mountains 6, 12, 13, 14, 18, 19, 20, 21

Neptune 26
nickel 5, 18, 24, 28
non-Newtonian fluid 23
North Pole 24, 25, 27
nuclear explosions 28

obsidian 22
oceanic crust 10, 12, 13, 14
ocean floor 16
oceans 8, 10, 11, 12, 13, 14, 18, 26
oil 16
ophiolite 12
outer core 4, 5, 6, 7, 24, 25, 26, 28, 29
oxygen 22

Pacific Ocean 13
Pangaea 10
plains 12
plates 12, 13, 18, 19, 20, 21
poles 24, 25, 27
pressure 4, 8, 16, 22, 23, 28
pressure waves 8, 9

quicksand 23

radiation 26
rain 10, 11, 16
resources 16, 17
rivers 14
rock cycle, the 15
rock samples 15
sandstone 14, 15
Saturn 26
sediment 14, 15
sedimentary rock 14
seismic waves 8, 9, 20
seismographs 8
shale 14
shear waves 8, 9, 29
shock waves 28
silica 5
silicon 22
slate 14
soil 26
solar flares 24
solar wind 24, 26
solids 8, 9, 18, 22, 23, 26, 27, 28, 29
South Pole 24, 25, 27
stored energy 20
subduction 12
Sun 8, 11, 16, 24, 26, 27, 28

tectonic plates 18, 19, 20, 21
temperature 4, 5, 8, 16, 22, 29
trench 12, 13

upper mantle 18, 20, 22
Uranus 26

valleys 12
vapour 10, 11
volcanic eruptions 18, 22, 26
volcanic mountains 21
volcanic rock 22
volcanoes 12, 18, 19, 22, 26

water 11, 16
water table, the 16
weathering 14
wells 16
winds 24

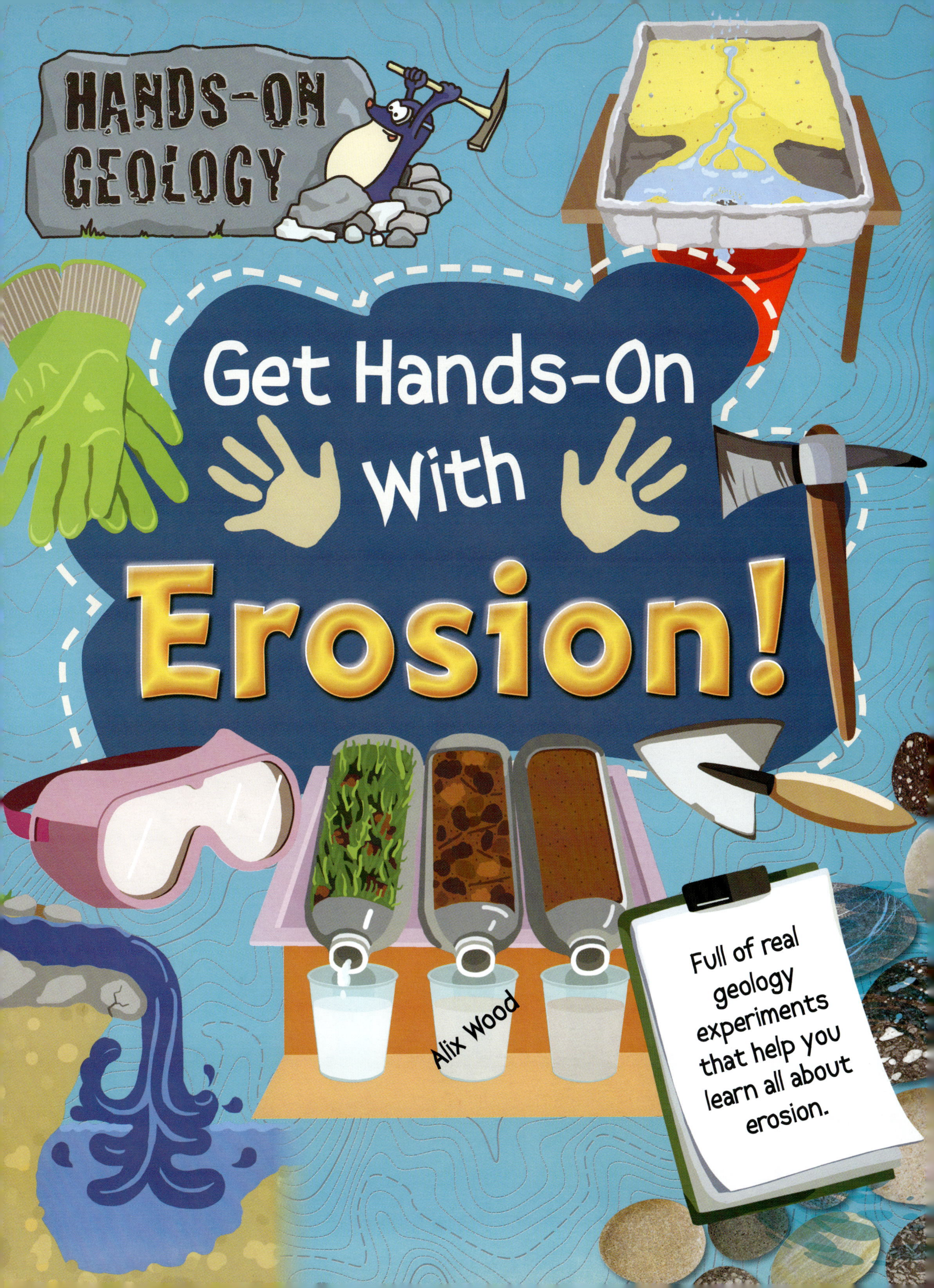
HANDS-ON GEOLOGY
Get Hands-On With
Erosion!
Alix Wood
Full of real geology experiments that help you learn all about erosion.

Contents

What Is Erosion? 36
Breaking Up Rocks By Weathering 38
Weathering By Water and Wind 40
Chemical Weathering 42
Rock-Breaking Plants and Animals 44
Erosion—Moving The Material 46
Erosion—The Power of Water 48
Erosion—Oceans and Ice 50
Earth's Forces 52
How Rivers Form a Valley 54
Dangerous Erosion! 56
Slowing Erosion 58
Creating New Landforms 60
Glossary 62
Further Information 63
Index 64

What Is Erosion?

Erosion is when natural forces such as water, wind, ice, and **gravity** transport worn rocks and soil from one place to another. This process is part of the rock cycle. Before material can be eroded, it needs to be weathered—broken down so it is small enough to be carried away. While strong stream currents might be able to move a boulder, a light breeze can only transport tiny fragments.

What forces do you think wore away this coast road?

The Rock Cycle

Once rock is weathered, the pieces get washed or blown away, often into rivers or the oceans. The pieces settle and form a layer known as **sediment**. This sediment gets pressed and compacted and sinks underground.

There, the sediment is heated and pressed into new rock, or melted by the high temperatures under Earth's surface to form a liquid rock known as **magma**.

Forces underground lift the newly-formed rock to the surface. In this way, all the **minerals** that make up Earth's rocks are constantly recycled!

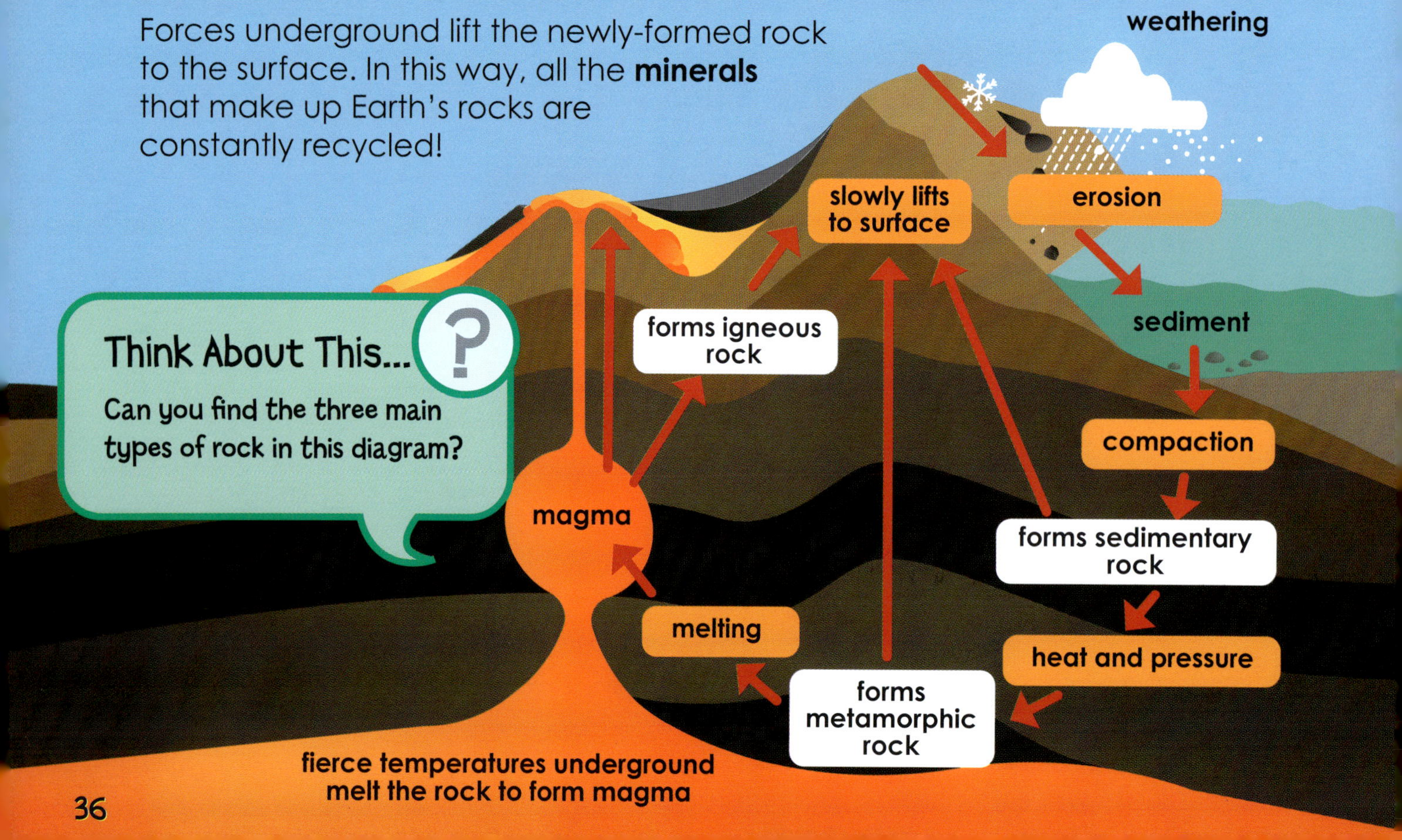

Think About This...

Can you find the three main types of rock in this diagram?

Weathering, Erosion, Deposition—What's the Difference?

Weathering is the process of breaking down rock and soil. If rock is broken down, but stays where it is, the process is called weathering.

Erosion is the process of carrying rock and soil away. Weathering helps erosion by breaking rock into small, easy to carry, pieces.

Deposition drops sediment in a new place. A river might move sediment downstream and then drop it (deposit it) there.

The ocean can weather and erode rock at the same time! Waves crash into the rock and break it into smaller pieces, and then carry those pieces out to sea.

HANDS-ON Break It, Move It, Drop It

You will need:
- a small bowl
- some pebbles
- some damp soil
- a flat dish
- a thin book
- a jug of water

Fill a bowl with a mixture of damp soil and pebbles. Tap the bowl to move the soil into all the gaps. Place a flat dish on top of the bowl. Holding the bowl and the dish, turn them both over. Lift the bowl, and your pebble mountain should now be on the dish.

Prop one end of the dish on a book, to form a slope. Slowly pour water on your mountain. You should see the water begin to BREAK up the soil. The river the water creates will MOVE the soil down the slope, and then DROP the soil at the bottom of the slope.

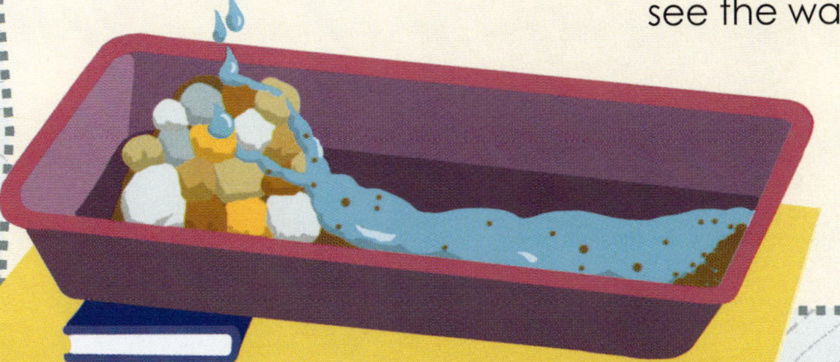

Breaking Up Rocks by Weathering

For material to be small enough to be carried by wind or water, it has to be broken into pieces. This process is known as weathering, because it is weather—the water and the temperature—that breaks the rock.

Types of Weathering

Rock is broken by **physical**, **chemical**, and **biological weathering**. Sometimes separately, but usually together, these processes change the structure of rock, making it softer and easily breakable.

Physical weathering

Weathering by wind, waves, water, and ice.

Water gets into cracks in rock, and freezes. As water freezes, it expands, forcing the crack open and splitting the rock.

Chemical weathering

Liquids or gases making changes to the chemicals that make up a rock.

Acid rain can dissolve soft rock. The limestone in this building has been eroded by acid rain.

Biological weathering

Weathering caused by plants and animals.

Limpets weather rock in two ways. They secrete an acid and they scratch at the rock as they feed.

HANDS-ON Find Local Weathering

You will need:

- adult help
- a notepad
- a pencil
- a camera

Ask a trusted adult to walk with you around your neighborhood to find examples of weathered rock. Good places to look are by rivers, lakes, the coast, or on windswept high ground. Look at old buildings, too. Can you find smooth rock, worn patterns, or cracking? Take photographs or make drawings of any examples that you find.

BE A GEOLOGIST

See How Ice Can Break Rocks

You Will Need:

- small balloon
- some water
- 3 cups of flour
- a bowl
- a bread board
- a freezer
- a little patience

The Geology:

You can tell water expands as it freezes by filling an ice cube tray with water. When the ice cubes have frozen they often stick out the top of the tray. When the water in your balloon freezes, it expands, just like water inside a crack in a rock would. Did your rock crack open under the pressure of the expanding ice?

How To Do The Experiment

To make your rock, fill a balloon with water until it is around the size of a golf ball. Squeeze any air out and tie the balloon closed.

Measure the flour into a bowl. Gradually add around 1.5 cups of water. Knead the mixture until it forms a soft dough.

Roll out a tennis ball-size lump of dough, a quarter of an inch (half a cm) thick. Place the balloon on the dough and carefully wrap the dough around it, smoothing any cracks. Leave it to dry. This may take a couple of days. Once dry, put it in the freezer overnight.

Can you predict what will happen? Take the rock out and have a look. What did the water in the balloon do?

Weathering by Water and Wind

Physical weathering by wind, waves, and water, change the **landscape** of our coastlines. Coastal areas tend to have strong winds, and waves pick up and throw rock as they crash onto the shore. Wind causes weathering in deserts, too, Strong winds pick up particles of sand and blast the surface of rock as they whistle by. Wind also causes rocks to rub against each other, smoothing their surfaces.

Worn Smooth by Flowing Water

When rocks weather each other by rubbing together this is known as **abrasion**. Rocks in a riverbed are worn smooth by abrasion as the **current** repeatedly knocks them into one another.

Broken Up by Salt

Waves hurl salt water into the cliff faces. Salt in seawater can force rock apart. How? Seawater gets washed into cracks and holes in the rock. In hot countries where the water **evaporates** quickly it leaves salt **deposits** behind. The deposits build up over time, and start to press outward, eventually breaking the rock.

Strong wind and seawater over the years have eroded the coast of Heping Island, Taiwan, forming these interesting shaped rocks. The weathered sandstone contains hundreds of **fossils**, too.

HANDS-ON Dissolving Rock

You will need:

- water
- some salt
- a piece of chalk
- a plate
- a teaspoon

Many minerals can be dissolved by water. Put a small pile of salt on a plate. Drop some water onto the salt using a teaspoon. What happens? Try the same experiment with a stick of chalk. Leave it in the water overnight. What happens?

BE A GEOLOGIST
Making and Weathering Mud Pies

You Will Need:

- a bucket of garden soil
- some water
- sandpaper
- eye protection
- spray bottle
- a small container
- an outside space
- a notepad and pencil
- a little patience

How To Do The Experiment

To make your mud pies, add water to the soil until wet, but not runny. Press a handful of mud into a patty. Make around five or six as you will use some of them later in the book. Leave them to dry for 2 - 3 days in a warm place.

Mimic weathering by wind-blown sand by rubbing some sandpaper over a dry mud pie. Wear eye protection as the dust can irritate your eyes. Try rubbing at different speeds and pressures. Try different grades of paper, too. Record your results.

Try spraying a mud pie with water. Spray it from different angles, and then concentrate on just one spot. Record what happens.

This one might be messy so cover up. Place a mud pie in a container and cover it with water. Then mimic the action of waves by rocking the container back and forth. Record what happens.

The Geology:

Your dried mud pies behave very like rock would under the same circumstances, but over many years.

Chemical Weathering

Chemical weathering is when water or gases make changes to the chemicals that make up a rock. Water can dissolve a mineral, or add water to a mineral, or react with a mineral. Gases, such as oxygen, can alter a rock's chemistry, too. For instance, oxygen caused this magnetite (right) to rust.

How does a rock rust? **Oxygen** in the air reacts with iron in some rock to form iron oxide, or rust. Iron oxide is a different color and much softer than the original rock. The reaction happens even faster if water or salt is present.

The amount of rust in an old rock can tell geologists how much oxygen was in the atmosphere long ago.

HANDS-ON Experiment With Rust

You will need:

- some fine steel wool from a paint store (dish-washing steel wool does not work as well)
- 3 glasses
- some water
- salt
- paper labels
- a notepad and pencil

Steel is a combination of iron and carbon. When iron is exposed to the air it starts to rust. Try this experiment to watch rust in action, and see if water or salt water speeds up the reaction.

Fill two of the glasses with water. Add salt to one of them. Write labels for each glass.

Tear the steel wool into three and place a piece in each glass. Observe what happens each day in your notebook. Which wool rusted the fastest? What conditions do you think will cause rock to rust quickly?

Think About This...

Adding salt to water causes **particles** to move more easily than they do in pure water. Do you think that will make the steel wool rust faster?

Water

Salt Water

Air

When **carbon dioxide**, **sulfur**, and **nitrogen** in the air react with water they cause **acid rain**. Acid rain breaks down some types of rock, such as marble, chalk, and limestone. Acid rain helps create caves. It also creates an unusual rocky landscape called **karst**.

Karst is an area of limestone full of holes and caves. One of the most spectacular examples is the Stone Forest, near Kunming, China. The limestone has been worn away to form a landscape of hundreds of sharp, rocky towers.

The Stone Forest, Kunming, China

BE A GEOLOGIST
Make Your Own Chalk Cave

You Will Need:

- large piece of natural chalk or a big stick of pavement chalk
- vinegar
- a teaspoon

The Geology:

Chalk is made of a type of limestone. Acid in the vinegar reacts with the chalk, dissolving it and producing carbon dioxide gas. The same process happens when acid in **groundwater** dissolves limestone.

How To Do The Experiment

Scratch a small hole in the chalk using the end of the teaspoon. Then use the teaspoon to drop some vinegar into the hole. The vinegar will react with the chalk, and you should see small bubbles appear.

Once there are no more bubbles, pour away the old vinegar and add some fresh vinegar. Repeat this until your cave is the size you want.

Where do you think the chalk goes in this experiment?

Rock-Breaking Plants and Animals

Have you ever seen a sidewalk cracked by the roots of a tree? **Biological weathering** is a type of weathering caused by plants and animals.

Roots

When plants grow in holes and cracks in rock, their roots exert pressure on rock as they grow. Known as wedging, the roots eventually expand the gaps until the rock splits apart.

Fungi and Bacteria

Some biological weathering causes chemical changes. **Lichen**, fungus, and mold produce rock-eating acid. Dead roots and leaves release carbon as they rot—which, mixed with water, forms a weak acid. Some bacteria remove nitrogen from minerals in rock. This weakens the rock, making it more easily weathered by wind and water.

Animals

Some types of clam burrow into solid rock. The chemicals in animal poop and urine can also break down minerals in rock. Animals walking on rocky slopes can cause rocks to slip and scrape against each other. Burrowing animals bring rocks to the surface to be weathered by other agents.

Think About This...

Humans are a type of animal. Can you think of any ways that human activity might break up rock or cause it to weather?

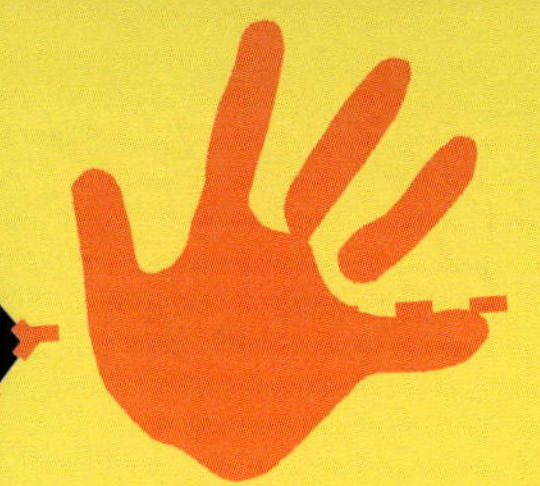

BE A GEOLOGIST
Spot Some Causes of Weathering

How many causes of weathering can you see in this picture? The answers are written below.

Answers: Fox poop and rotting leaves creating acids, mole hole bringing rock to the surface, goat and people disturbing rock as they walk, tractor disturbing rocks, tree roots cracking rock, lichen growing on rocks and producing acids.

Erosion—Moving The Material

Once weathering has broken rock down, the forces of erosion take over to move the material away. Water, wind, ice, and gravity can all move rocks, stone, or sand grains away from their location. Wind may only be able to move small particles, but it can move very large amounts of small particles! For example, wind created enormous **sand dunes** in the Gobi Desert, China that are over 1,300 feet (400 m) high!

Wind Erosion

Just as with weathering, more than one force can cause erosion in a place. Geologists believe wind erosion was one of the forces that shaped the Grand Canyon. Strong winds blow through the canyons, blowing particles into the water to be carried away.

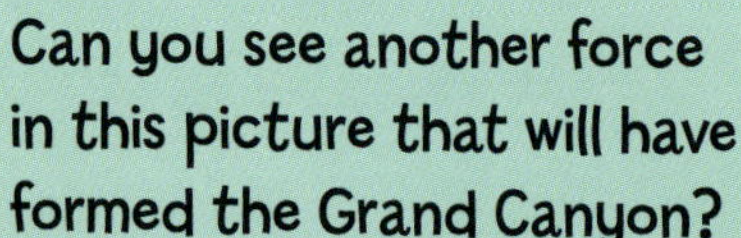

Think About This...

Can you see another force in this picture that will have formed the Grand Canyon?

HANDS-ON Make a Sand Dune

You will need:
- some newspaper
- sand
- a baking pan
- a straw

A sand dune is a hill of loose sand built by wind. They form when an obstruction stops the sand traveling past, and so it piles up. Try making a sand dune. Cover a table with newspaper. Pour sand into a baking pan. Press a rock into the sand. Hold a straw just above the sand and blow gently through it toward the rock. Remove the straw from your mouth between each breath so you don't breathe in sand. The sand will gradually form a sand dune around the rock. Experiment with different obstructions and see how your dunes change shape.

BE A GEOLOGIST
Make a Wind-Eroded Rock Formation

You Will Need:

adult help needed

- some damp sand
- a small bucket
- a hair dryer
- some flat rocks small enough to fit in the bucket
- a large cardboard box
- some thick card

The Geology:

Wind can carve channels and shapes in solid stone. Different rock types weather at different rates. Granite rock weathers slowly. Limestone is easily weathered. Rocks that resist weathering remain and form ridges or hills. The surrounding, less resistant rocks are worn away like the sand in this experiment.

How To Do The Experiment:

Design a rock formation by stacking some flat stones on top of each other. Place a handful of damp sand in the bottom of the bucket. Now rebuild your rock formation, from the top down, in the bucket. Pack damp sand around it to hold it in place as you build. Finish with a flat layer of damp sand.

This can get messy so you may want to do it outside. Put the cardboard box on its side. Place some thick card over the bucket. Turn the bucket upside down and then lift it off. Put the card, with the sandcastle on it, in the box.

Ask an adult to help you—anything electrical is dangerous, especially near water. Put the hair dryer on a low setting and point it at the sandcastle. You should see sand gradually eroding away as it dries and is blown to the back of the box. Increase the setting if nothing happens. Your rock formation should gradually start to appear.

Erosion—The Power of Water

Crashing waves, heavy rain, powerful waterfalls, and gushing rivers all help transport weathered rock. Water is the most common cause of erosion.

BE A GEOLOGIST
Water Erosion Experiments

You Will Need:

- a baking tray
- some soil
- a teaspoon
- water
- some books
- a cup
- a notebook and pencil
- spray bottle full of water
- a camera if you have one

The Geology:

Heavy rain loosens particles and transports them downhill. You will see brown water appear at the bottom of your slope, showing it is now full of eroded material.

On steep slopes the force of gravity means water will flow faster and may cause a mudslide. A sudden large amount of water causes the soil to saturate, meaning it cannot soak up any more liquid. This is how floods happen.

How To Do The Experiment

Form some damp soil into a slope at one end of a baking tray. Leave the other end free of soil. To see the effect of water erosion, try these experiments. Take notes, and make drawings or photograph what happens with each experiment.

Different types of rain
Create rain by dripping water on the soil using a teaspoon. Try dripping it on the same spot, and different spots. Then spray the soil. Spray from different angles. If your spray bottle has different settings, try them out. Take notes. Look at the area at the bottom of your slope. Does water appear there? What color is it?

Water on a slope
Rebuild your soil landscape. Pour away any excess water. Put some books under the soil end of the tray to create a slope. Repeat the drip and spray experiments and compare your results.

Floods
Rebuild your soil landscape. Tip a cup of water, all at once, on the soil. What happens?

Waterfalls

Waterfalls are created where areas of hard rock and soft rock meet in a riverbed. The soft rock erodes more quickly, forming a step. The force of the falling water creates a plunge pool. The overhanging ledge of the waterfall will eventually collapse, and the fallen rock erodes the pool even more. Waterfalls constantly move upriver as more and more rock erodes.

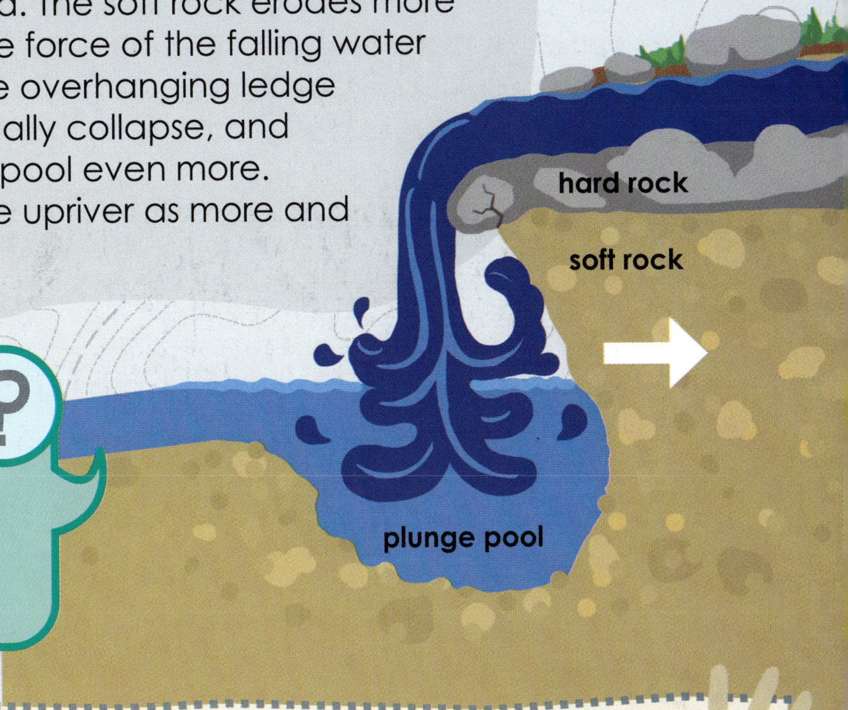

hard rock

soft rock

plunge pool

Think About This...

Why do you think earthquakes, landslides, and volcanoes might also cause waterfalls to form?

HANDS-ON Erode Your Own Waterfall

You will need:

- a dish pan
- a large pile of sand
- a small chopping board or similar
- water
- a jug

Make a large sand pile in the dish pan. The sand represents the soft rock layer. Push the board into one side of the sand pile, about half-way up, angled down a little. The board represents the hard rock layer.

Pour water onto the same side of the sand pile that you pushed the board into. Watch what happens.

The water will flow down the sandy slope, and gradually wear away the top, soft layer. As the water meets the board it will fall over its edge and start to cut back in as it falls onto the softer rock below. As you keep pouring water, you should see your waterfall get bigger and a plunge pool start to develop. You may want to bail out some of the excess water at the bottom of the bowl from time to time, so your sand doesn't get washed away.

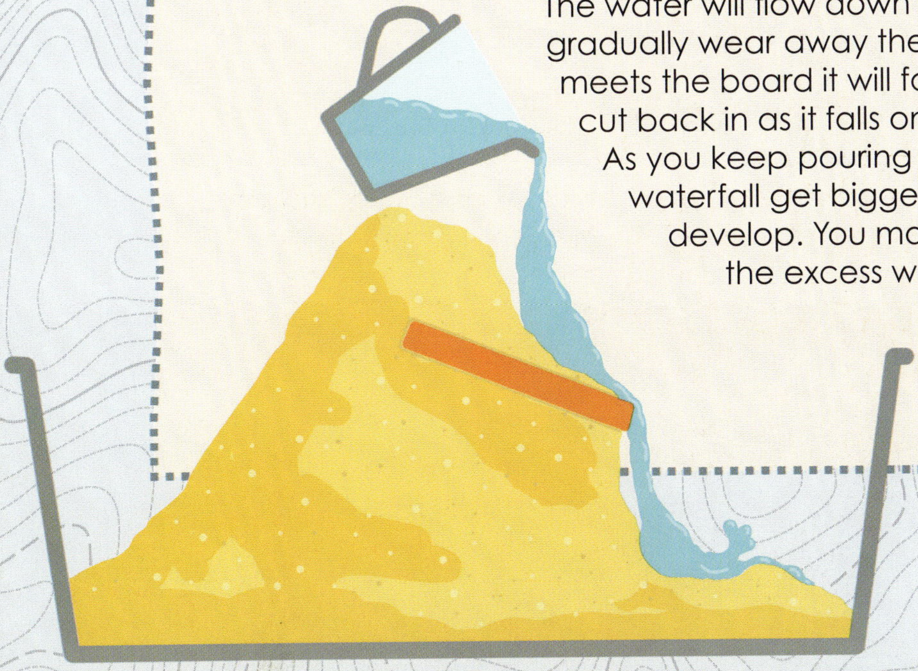

Erosion—Oceans and Ice

The power of the ocean waves and huge, moving slabs of ice can make dramatic changes to the landscape as they move rock from one place to another.

Shaping Our Coastlines

Waves crashing into ocean cliffs gradually wear away softer rock to form bays. The areas of harder rock left jutting out to sea are known as headland.

HANDS-ON Erode a Coastline

You will need:

- some sand
- some rocks
- a deep dish
- some water

Place a rock halfway down each side of the dish. Then form a straight coastline of sand between the two rocks. Pour water into the dish. Pat the water to create ocean waves. Watch your bay erode and your two headlands take shape.

Waves force their way into cracks in cliffs, bringing sand that grinds the rock to create caves. Spray pushes blow holes in cave roofs. Waves can wear right through headland, to form an arch. Large arches collapse, leaving a column known as a stack. When a stack collapses, it forms a stump.

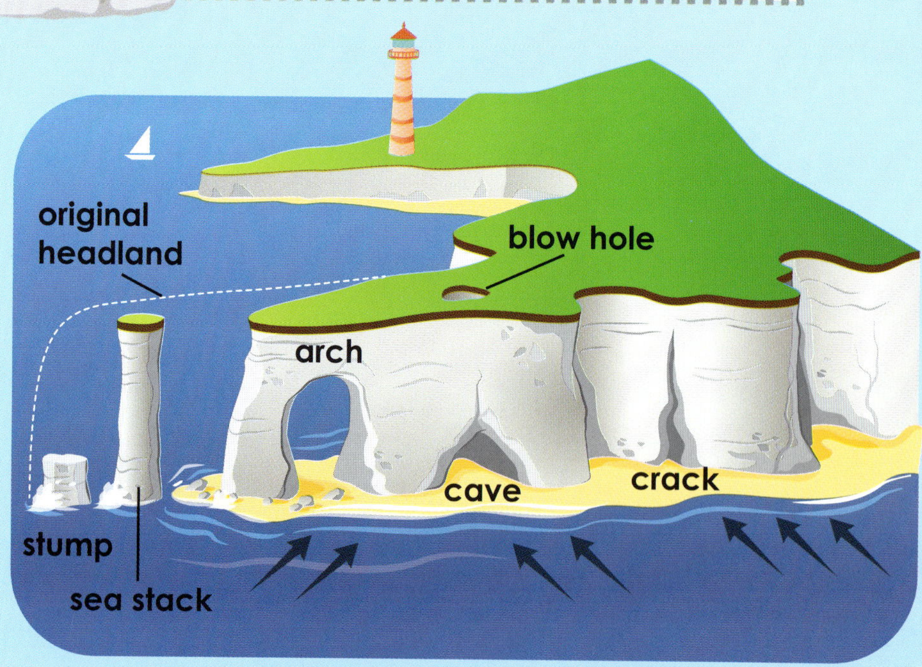

Enormous Moving Slabs of Ice

A **glacier** is a slow-moving river of ice that slides along Earth's surface. Glaciers can move huge boulders great distances and create vast, smooth "U" shaped valleys.

Glaciers move material in three ways.

- Melt water freezes around cracked rock and then moves with the glacier, **plucking** the rock with it.
- Rock, frozen into the base of the glacier, scrapes the bedrock, and this abrasion moves other rock.
- Water in cracks in the bedrock freezes and thaws, eventually breaking off pieces of rock which move with the glacier.

plucking

freeze-thaw

abrasion

Think About This...

Which type of erosion do you think can move the largest rocks: Wind, water or glacier?

BE A GEOLOGIST
How a Glacier Moves Boulders

You Will Need:

- a ziplock bag
- some water
- a freezer
- a tray of soil
- 2 or 3 small rocks
- a book

How To Do The Experiment

Put the rocks into a ziplock bag and then fill the bag with water. Seal it and place it in the freezer overnight. Put a layer of soil in the tray. Prop up one end of the tray on a book to create a slope. Take your ice block out of the bag and place it at the top of the slope. Record where the rocks are deposited once the ice melts.

The Geology:

As the glacier melts it will transport rock and soil down the slope with it.

Earth's Forces

Forces from deep inside Earth can cause weathering, and erosion, too. Earth is made up of a series of **tectonic plates**, a little like a jigsaw. These plates move slightly as they float on the semi-liquid layer beneath the Earth's crust. When two plates stick and then suddenly release this can cause an earthquake.

During an earthquake, rocks caught between moving plates may fracture into smaller fragments. Some underground fragments may make their way to the surface. The powerful shaking causes rocks on the surface to rub together. It can also cause **landslides**.

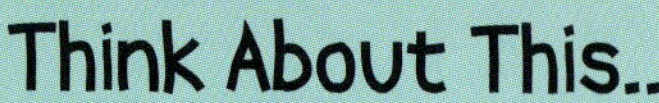

Think About This...

Do you know the name of the force that causes things to fall downward?

Landslides

Mudslides and landslides occur because of the pull of gravity on loose earth on a slope. Earthquakes, heavy rain, snow, or ice, poor construction and leaking underground pipes can all cause landslides. Rocks can be shattered into fragments as they fall down the slope. They will also rub against each other as they roll or slide.

HANDS-ON Earthquake!

You will need:

- a large book
- a rectangular cake tin
- four bouncy balls or marbles
- two large rubber bands
- two dry mud pies from page 9

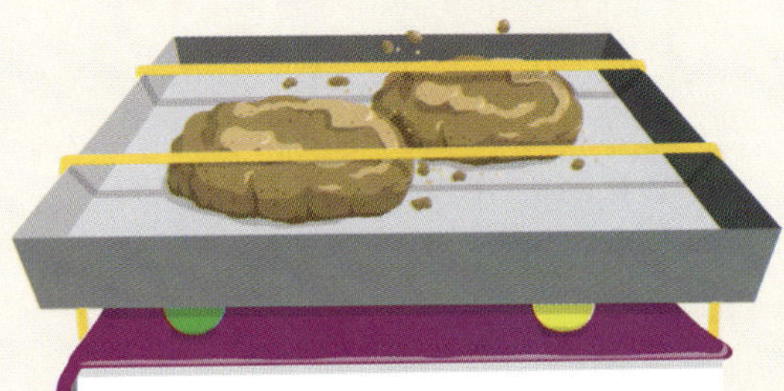

Experiment breaking up rock with earthquakes by making a shake table. Place four balls between a book and a cake tin. Wrap the rubber bands around the book and tin to hold everything in place. Wobbling the cake tin should make it shake as it rolls on the balls.

Put the mud pies in the tin and then shake it, like an earthquake. Do the mud pies start to weather? With how much force, and for how long, do you need to shake before they really start to break up?

BE A GEOLOGIST
How Does Rain Cause Landslides?

You Will Need:

- a plastic dish pan
- newspaper
- some mud
- spray bottle and water
- model houses
- small stones

The Geology:

Water adds weight to the slope and lowers the strength of the material so it is less able to withstand the force of gravity.

How To Do The Experiment

Fill one end of the dish pan with scrunched up balls of newspaper. Press mud onto the newspaper to form a steep hillside. Place some model houses and stones on your slope. To create a landslide, spray water onto the hillside, a little at a time.

How much water did it take before the mud started slipping down the hill? What happened to your model houses? Did your stones crash into each other?

How Rivers Form a Valley

Most valleys and canyons are formed by rivers. The flowing water erodes the surrounding rock and wears it into sand and **silt**. River valleys are always changing as the river continually wears away the land through which they flow.

The river twists and turns around stones and other obstructions. Areas of slower and faster water movement cause the river to start to flow from side to side. The faster-moving water on the outside of a bend erodes more, and gradually forms a river cliff.

Water moves slower on the inside of the bend. Deposited material often forms a beach. Erosion on the outer bank and deposits on the inner bank causes bends in the river known as **meanders**.

Rivers begin high up in the mountains. As they flow quickly downhill they cut a notch into the landscape. Rocks that fall into the fast-flowing river add to the erosion. The river becomes wider and deeper, creating a V-shaped valley.

Think About This...

Not all valleys are formed by rivers. Glaciers and movement in Earth's plates can cause valleys to form, too.

Oxbow lakes form from old bends in a river. When a river floods, the water sometimes finds a shorter route, and goes across the bend rather than around it. The bend becomes a lake, separated from the river by deposited rock and silt.

Flooded areas can become very **fertile**. Sand, silt, minerals, and organic matter are brought to the areas when the river floods, which improves the soil.

HANDS-ON Make a River Valley

You will need:

- a tray of sand
- some small rocks
- a jug of water

Create a mountain landscape in a tray of sand. Slowly pour water from the jug over a mountain. Watch as your river valley forms, pulling sand and stones along with the flow of water.

How much force does your river need to move larger rock? Where does it deposit rock, and why? Move the rocks around. Does that alter the course of your river? Slow the flow of water. Can your river move rock now, or just sand?

Dangerous Erosion!

Erosion is a natural process, and it can be good for the environment. Erosion helps cleanse the soil of nutrient-less dirt. It helps form incredible landscapes. But, erosion can cause all kinds of problems, too.

What's The Problem With Erosion?

- Eroded material can clog rivers and canals, causing flooding. Floods damage homes and farmland.

- Erosion can wash away good soil making it impossible to grow crops. The world is losing soil faster than it can be formed again, which may mean we cannot grow enough food.

- Buried poisonous and plastic waste from old landfill sites can get exposed and washed into our oceans and rivers. Harmful fertilizers and other chemicals can get washed into low land, rivers, and oceans, too.

- Erosion makes some land unstable. Whole villages have been lost over cliffs because of erosion. Large rock falls, sinkholes, or landslides can bury roads or buildings.

- Rising sea levels and flooding due to climate change have increased soil and coastal erosion. If we tackle climate change we will help slow dangerous erosion.

Coastal erosion!

Sinkholes!

Flooding!

Think About This...

Can you think of ways we can prevent these types of dangerous erosion?

How Do Sinkholes Happen?

Sinkholes occur when underground water dissolves soft rock such as salt and limestone. They develop underground for a long time before the hole appears. Water very slowly erodes the rocks and minerals. The surface above collapses, and a hole opens up. Drilling, mining, and broken water pipes can also cause sinkholes. Some sinkholes can be hundreds of miles (kms) wide and deep and swallow whole buildings!

BE A GEOLOGIST
Create a Sinkhole in a Paper Cup

You Will Need:

- sugar or flour
- sand or soil
- a toilet roll tube
- a plastic cup
- a small piece of sponge
- a bowl of water
- a tray

The Geology:

In this experiment, the sugar represents easily eroded minerals. The sinkhole appears as the sugar is dissolved by the underground water quicker than the surrounding material is.

How To Do The Experiment

Poke a hole in the bottom of a plastic cup. Put a piece of sponge in the cup, and place a toilet roll tube on the sponge. Place the cup on a tray, to catch any spills. Pour sand or soil carefully around the tube. Then pour sugar or flour inside the tube.

Carefully remove the tube and you'll have a "soft rock" layer of sugar in the middle of your "hard rock" layer of sand. Cover the top with a little sand to represent the solid-looking ground over a sinkhole.

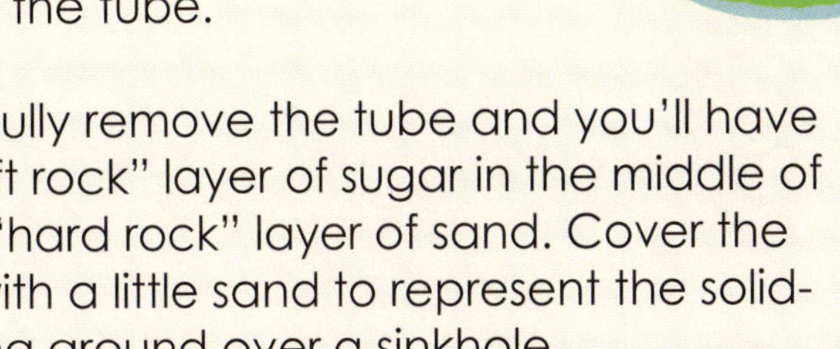

To mimic the underground water, get a jug of water. Hold the cup in the jug, just under the water level, so a little water starts to spill into the cup. Then quickly lift the cup back out. You should see a sink hole appear as the sugar dissolves.

Slowing Erosion

We can't stop erosion, but we can slow it down. Along many coastlines, **climate change** is causing increased erosion. This means people living by the coast may lose their homes to the sea and we might lose important coastal environments like sand dunes.

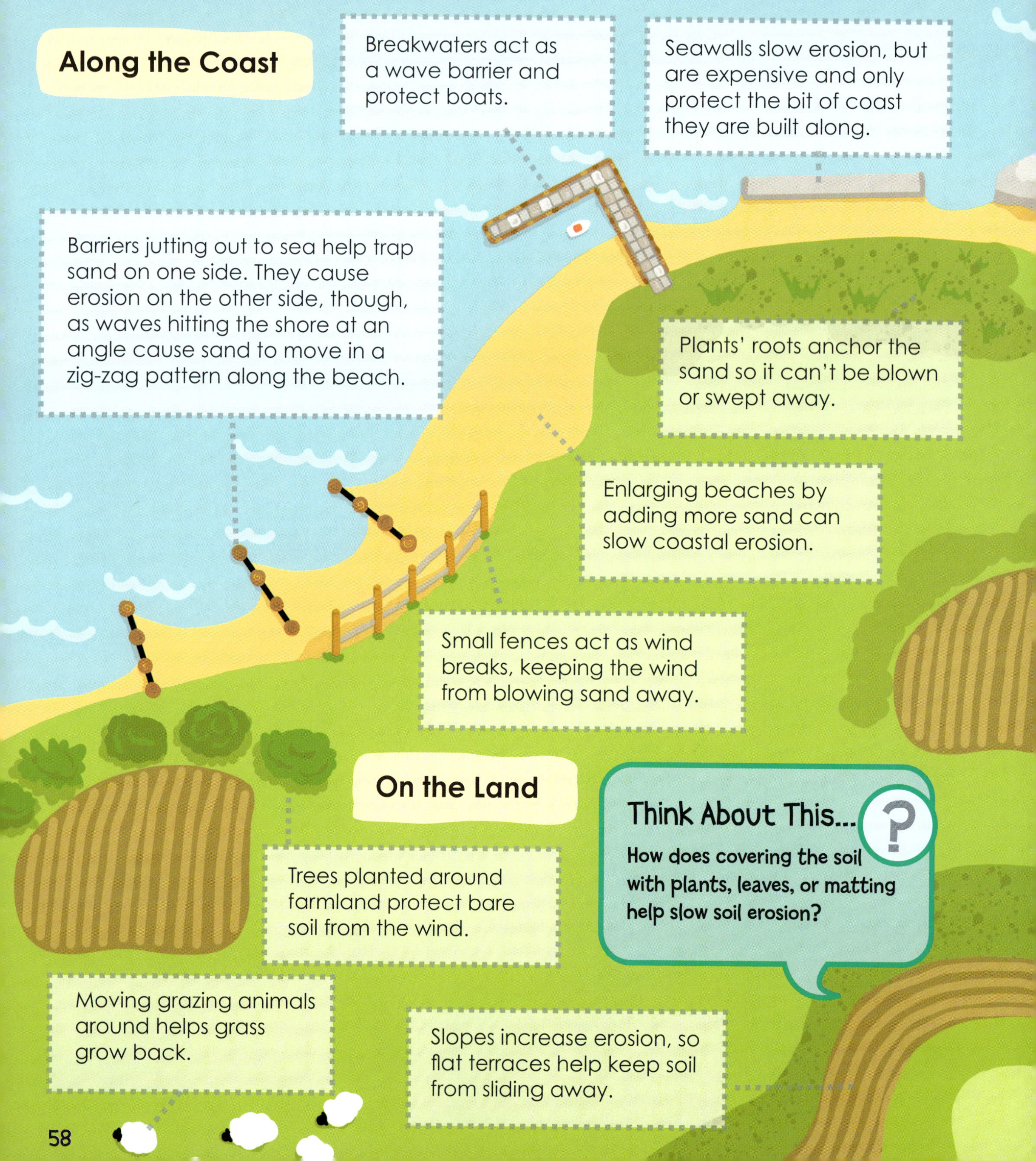

Along the Coast

Breakwaters act as a wave barrier and protect boats.

Seawalls slow erosion, but are expensive and only protect the bit of coast they are built along.

Barriers jutting out to sea help trap sand on one side. They cause erosion on the other side, though, as waves hitting the shore at an angle cause sand to move in a zig-zag pattern along the beach.

Plants' roots anchor the sand so it can't be blown or swept away.

Enlarging beaches by adding more sand can slow coastal erosion.

Small fences act as wind breaks, keeping the wind from blowing sand away.

On the Land

Trees planted around farmland protect bare soil from the wind.

Moving grazing animals around helps grass grow back.

Slopes increase erosion, so flat terraces help keep soil from sliding away.

Think About This...

How does covering the soil with plants, leaves, or matting help slow soil erosion?

BE A GEOLOGIST
Test Which Materials Slow Soil Erosion

You Will Need:

adult help needed

- three cups
- some soil
- a tray
- a few books
- a small piece of turf
- some dead leaves
- three large plastic bottles
- an outdoor step
- a jug of water

How To Do The Experiment:

Ask an adult to help you cut a large rectangle from the side of each of the plastic bottles. Do not cut off the neck or base. Place the bottles on their sides in a line on a tray, with the necks hanging over the edge. Put soil in two bottles. Put a layer of dead leaves on top of the soil in one bottle. Fill the last bottle with turf, along with its roots and soil. Put the tray on a step. Place a cup under each bottle's spout on the step below. If the bottles roll, wedge them with a few books.

Can you predict which bottle will erode the most soil? Make sure the cups are under the spouts. Carefully pour water into each bottle. You need to pour enough so water will come out of the bottle top, but not overflow the cups.

Examine the water in the cups. Which bottle eroded the most soil? Which cup has the cleanest water? Did that match your predictions?

The Geology:

Bare soil erodes quite easily. Adding a layer of leaves acts a little like an umbrella, protecting the soil from being washed away by rainfall. The grass protects the soil in the same way. The roots also help hold the soil in place and they soak up a lot of the water.

Try propping the back of the tray on some books so the bottles form a slope. Does that change how much soil is eroded? Can you see why hill farmers make terraces?

Creating New Landforms

After material has been eroded, where does it go and what happens to it? Eroded material is eventually deposited by water, wind, or ice. As it settles, it can create new landforms. Landforms are natural features on the surface of Earth.

Wind deposits sand along this fence, creating a sand dune.

What causes material to be deposited?

Flowing water will eventually slow, or evaporate, winds die down, and glaciers melt. Anything that slows down water, or the force of the wind, will cause deposition. While erosion can destroy landscapes, deposition can create new ones.

Think About This...

Can you think of any landforms that are created by deposition?

HANDS-ON Explore Glacier Landforms

You will need:

- a paper cup
- dirt and gravel
- water
- a freezer
- 2 cups of flour
- cooking spray
- a baking tray

Put a little dirt and gravel in a paper cup and then fill it to the top with water. Place it in a freezer overnight. Spray a baking sheet with cooking spray. Pour two cups of flour onto the tray and spread it out to make an even surface. Take your ice "glacier" out of the cup and place it at one end of the tray. Press down and push the glacier across the tray.

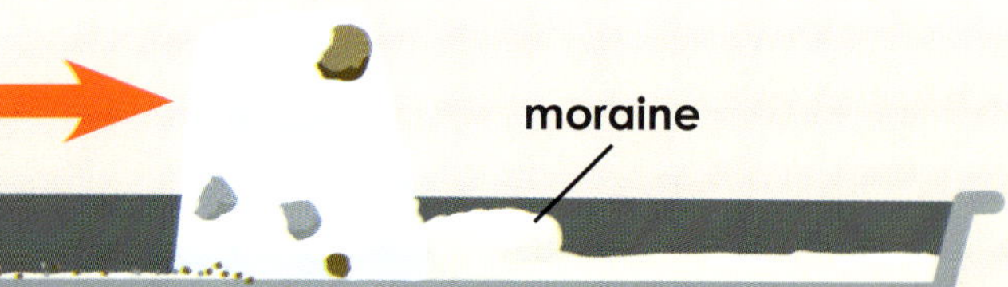

Examine the landforms it left in the flour. Glaciers create a valley, scraping the ground with rocks caught up in the ice. The mounds that form to the front and sides are known as **moraines**.

Sediment Forming Deltas

Rivers always flow toward a larger body of water. A delta is a wetland area that forms when a river slows as it empties into an ocean or lake. Sediment dropped at the mouth of the river builds up to form the delta. The river cuts small channels through the sediment.

BE A GEOLOGIST

Make a Delta Using a Stream Table

You Will Need:

adult help needed

- foil turkey pan
- scissors
- a bucket
- some books
- sand, small dead leaves and twigs, and gravel
- a small watering can
- a notebook and pencil
- a large trash bag

How To Do The Experiment

Cut a penny-size hole in the bottom of a turkey pan, near the edge of a short side. Mix 3 parts sand, 1 part dead leaves, and 1 part gravel. Put the mixture in the pan, opposite the hole, so it covers about two-thirds of the pan. Prop the soil end of the pan on some books. Hang the other end over the edge of a table. Cover the floor with the trash bag to catch any drips, and place a bucket under the hole.

Hold the watering can a ruler's height above the pan. Pour water onto the top of the slope. Make sure your bucket is catching the drips. A stream should start to form in the sand. In your notebook, draw and label any landforms that form.

The Geology:

A river's shape changes depending on the type of soil and rock, the angle of the slope, and the amount of water. Try changing these things and see what happens. Where does your river landscape deposit sediment? Did you create a delta? Can you make your river alter its course?

Glossary

abrasion a rubbing, grinding, or wearing away by friction.

acid rain rain with increased acidity caused by its environment.

bacteria any of a group of single-celled microorganisms that live in soil, water, the bodies of plants and animals.

biological weathering changes to exposed rocks, minerals, and soil caused by living things.

carbon dioxide a heavy colorless gas formed especially by the burning and breaking down of organic substances, is absorbed from the air by plants.

chemical weathering changes to exposed rocks, minerals, and soil caused by chemical reactions.

climate change a long-term change in the average weather patterns.

corrode to be eaten away by degrees.

current a body of water or air moving in a definite direction.

deposition the action or process of depositing.

deposits something laid or thrown down.

evaporates to pass off into vapor from a liquid state.

fertile producing vegetation or crops plentifully.

fossils traces or prints or the remains of a plant or animal of a past age preserved in earth or rock.

fungi living things that lack chlorophyll, are parasitic or live on dead or decaying organic matter.

glacier a large body of ice moving slowly down a slope or valley or spreading outward on a land surface.

gravity a force of attraction between particles or bodies that occurs because of their mass.

groundwater the water found underground in the cracks and spaces in soil, sand and rock.

karst limestone landscape which has been eroded, producing ridges.

landscape the land that can be seen in one glance.

landslides the slipping down of a mass of rocks or earth on a steep slope.

lichen plantlike living things made up of an alga and a fungus.

magma molten rock material inside Earth.

meanders a turn or winding of a stream.

minerals solid chemical compounds that occur naturally in the form of crystals.

moraines piles of earth and stones carried and deposited by a glacier.

nitrogen a colorless, tasteless, odorless element that occurs as a gas. It makes up 78 percent of the atmosphere and forms a part of all living tissues.

oxygen a colorless, tasteless, odorless gas which forms about 21 percent of the atmosphere, and is necessary for life.

particles one of the very small parts of matter.

physical weathering changes to exposed rocks, minerals, and soil that affects their physical appearance.

plucking quickly removing something from its place.

sand dunes hills of sand near an ocean or in a desert formed by the wind.

sediment material such as stones and sand deposited by water, wind, or glaciers.

silt a soil made from very small particles of sediment from water.

sulfur a nonmetallic element.

tectonic plates large pieces of the surface of Earth that move separately.

weathering the action of the forces of nature that changes exposed rocks, minerals, and soil.

Further Information

Museums and Places to Visit

Visitors' centers. Your area may have caves, river canyons, wetlands, saltmarshes or desert visitor centers, where you could find information about erosion.

Local farms or farming museums. Farmers are very knowledgeable about the soil. There may be farms in your area that could show you how they help stop soil erosion.

Contact climate change action groups. Ask if you can join a local group that helps combat climate change.

Useful Websites

This Science for Kids Club website is packed with useful, easy-to-understand information about erosion.
https://www.scienceforkidsclub.com/erosion.html

A National Geographic webpage with information on erosion and links to related topics. It features clickable links to definitions of the terms used on the page.
https://www.nationalgeographic.org/encyclopedia/erosion/

A Learning Junction video cartoon with everything you need to know about soil erosion and how to prevent it.
https://www.youtube.com/watch?v=qNTOq1uEObc

Books to Read

Brannon, Cecelia H. *A Look at Erosion and Weathering (Rock Cycle)* New York, NY: Enslow Publishing, 2016.

Slipe, Nicole. *Restoring Muddy Creek (Smithsonian: Informational Text)*. Huntington Beach, CA: Teacher Created Materials, 2018.

Index

abrasion 40, 51
acid 38, 43, 44
acid rain 38, 43
animals 38, 44, 45, 58
arches 50
atmosphere 42

bacteria 44
barriers 58
bays 50
bends 54, 55
biological weathering 38, 44, 45
blow holes 50
breakwaters 58
buildings 38, 39, 56, 57
burrowing 44, 45

canals 56
canyons 54
carbon 42, 44
carbon dioxide 43
caves 43, 50
chalk 41, 43
chemicals 42, 44, 56
chemical weathering 38, 42
clams 44
cliffs 40, 50, 54, 56
climate change 56, 58
coast 39, 40
coastal erosion 56, 58
coastlines 40, 50, 58
construction 52
cracks 38, 39, 40, 44, 45, 51
crops 56
crust 52
currents 36, 40

deltas 61
deposits 40, 54, 55, 60, 61
deposition 36, 60
desert 40
dissolving 41, 43, 57
drilling 57

earthquakes 49, 52, 53
evaporation 40, 60
expanding 38, 39, 44

farmland 56, 58
fertilizers 56
floods 48, 55, 56
forces 52, 53, 55
fossils 40
freezing 38, 39, 51, 60
fungi 44

gases 38, 42, 43
glaciers 50, 51, 60
Gobi Desert China 46
Grand Canyon the 46
granite 47
grass 58, 59
gravity 36, 46, 52, 53
grazing 58
groundwater 43, 57

headland 50
Heping Taiwan 40
hills 47

ice 36, 38, 39, 46, 50, 51, 52, 60
igneous rock 36
iron 42
iron oxide 42

karst 43

lakes 39, 55, 61
landfill sites 56
landforms 60, 61
landscape 40, 43, 50, 54, 55, 56, 60, 61
landslides 49, 52, 53, 56
leaks 52, 57
leaves 44, 45, 58, 59, 61
lichen 44, 45
limestone 38, 43, 46, 57
limpets 38

magma 36
magnetite 42
marble 43
matting 58
meanders 54
metamorphic rock 36
minerals 36, 42, 44, 55, 57
mining 57
mold 44
moraines 60
mountains 37, 54, 55
mudslides 52

nitrogen 43, 44

oceans 36, 37, 50, 56, 61
organic matter 55
oxbow lakes 55
oxygen 42

particles 42, 46
physical weathering 38, 40
plants 38, 44, 45, 58, 59
plowing 45
plunge pools 49
pressure 39, 44

rain 48, 52, 59
ridges 47
rivers 36, 39, 40, 48, 49, 54, 55, 56, 61
rock cycle the 36
rock formations 47
roots 44, 45, 58, 59
rust 42

salt 40, 41, 42, 57
sand 40, 41, 46, 47, 49, 50, 54, 55, 57, 58
sand dunes 46, 58, 60
sandstone 40
sea levels 56
seawalls 58
seawater 40
sediment 36, 37, 61
sedimentary rock 36
shake table 53
silt 54, 55
sinkholes 56, 57
slopes 48, 49, 51, 52, 53, 54, 55, 58, 59
smoothing 39, 40
snow 52
soil 36, 37, 41, 48, 51, 55, 56, 58, 59, 61
soil erosion 58, 59
stacks 50
Stone Forest China 43
stumps 50
sulfur 43

tectonic plates 52
temperature 36, 38
terraces 58
hawing 51
trees 58

urine 44

valleys 51, 54, 55, 60, 61
volcanoes 49

water 36, 37, 38, 40, 41, 42, 44, 46, 51, 53, 54, 55, 59, 60, 61
waterfalls 48, 49
waves 37, 38, 40, 41, 48, 50, 58
weathering 36, 37, 38, 40, 41, 44, 45, 46, 47, 48, 52, 53
wind 36, 38, 39, 40, 41, 44, 46, 47, 51, 58, 60
wetland 61
windbreaks 58